Journey to the Empty Tomb

BIBLICAL EXPLORATIONS

Journey to the Empty Tomb

Paula Gooder

CANTERBURY
PRESS

Norwich

© Paula Gooder 2014

First published in 2014 by the Canterbury Press Norwich
Editorial office
3rd Floor, Invicta House,
108–114 Golden Lane,
London EC1Y 0TG

Canterbury Press is an imprint of Hymns Ancient & Modern Ltd
(a registered charity)
13A Hellesdon Park Road, Norwich,
Norfolk NR6 5DR, UK

www.canterburypress.co.uk

British Library Cataloguing in Publication data

A catalogue record for this book is available
from the British Library

978 1 84825 571 5

Typeset by Regent Typesetting
Printed and bound in Great Britain by
CPI Group (UK) Ltd, Croydon

Contents

CONTENTS

Prologue

The seed for this book was sown and then nurtured in two of the most iconic cities in Christian history. In January 2012 I was privileged to be invited to accompany the then Archbishop of Canterbury, Rowan Williams, on a pilgrimage to the Holy Land. It was a profoundly moving experience, and all those of us who went recount in different ways how the pilgrimage changed our lives and our relationship with God. One afternoon we sat together in Jerusalem on the roof of the hostel where we were staying and I was asked to reflect for a while on why, from the perspective of the New Testament and New Testament scholars, Jesus died.

In a subsequent conversation, the then Director of the Anglican Centre in Rome, David Richardson, suggested that the ideas we had begun to explore would make a rather good course. As a result, in March of the following year, I led a course in Rome at the Anglican Centre with the same title as this book. The primary question of the course was the same as the one we had raised in Jerusalem – Why did Jesus die?

Over the space of a week with a wonderful group of participants from many different places around the world, we explored the last week of Jesus' life in the pages of the Gospels, starting with Palm Sunday and ending at the resurrection. At the end of that week it seemed to me and to a number of others that I spoke to, that these ideas had further to go, and that people other than simply those who had been able to come on the course might appreciate the chance to explore the last week of Jesus' life in more detail.

The idea for this book was born and nurtured in Jerusalem and Rome: the two key cradles of early Christianity.

The book would never have taken the form it has, however, without two significant groups of people: my fellow pilgrims to the Holy Land and my fellow course participants in Rome. I dedicate this book to you all with love and gratitude for your wisdom, your inspiration and your willingness to be true companions on the way.

* * *

This book could be read in all sorts of ways. It aims to be 'academically devotional'. By this I mean that I use the insights of scholarship to understand the Gospel texts better, and by doing so attempt to reinspire and reinvigorate our devotional journeys with Jesus to the cross and beyond. It is designed for anyone who wants to explore the texts of the last week of Jesus' life in a little more detail. It is a 'semi-commentary' in that I am exploring the texts in order, but I attempt to do this differently by providing continuous text that is easier to read than many commentaries are, supplemented by boxes which pull out details where necessary. It is not exhaustive – a book of this length simply cannot aim to be. As a result there will be details, and even whole passages, that cannot be pursued as well as they might.

What is covered are things that I think are interesting; my apologies in advance where you disagree with me on what counts as interesting. What this small book really aims to do is whet your appetite again for reading these passages in detail and reflecting on what the Gospel writers were attempting to communicate in the way that they wrote.

At the end of each section are a few paragraphs of reflection based around thoughts and ideas that my study of the passages has evoked in me. Again these are not exhaustive and you may find that you have entirely different reflections yourself. In a similar way at the end of each chapter is a prayer/meditation, which again reflect ideas that have occurred to me as I wrote. Some will appreciate them, others may not; please engage with them or not as is helpful to you.

Some people will want to read the book early on in Lent to help them get new ideas for what they might say in the services of Holy Week and Easter; others will want to read it through Lent to help them prepare personally for Easter; others still may want to read the book in Holy Week itself to help them focus on the events of the last week of Jesus' life in the actual week that we commemorate them. Alternatively you may dip in and out, just looking at the sections that interest you. (If you want to use the material in this book as a Lent course I have added questions for discussion right at the end of the book and a suggestion of how the material could be used in the context of a study group.)

Given this, I have arranged the material into five chapters. I cannot stress strongly enough that the chapters do not fit the actual days of Holy Week, not least because it is impossible to decide which events described in the Gospels as taking place after the triumphal entry and before the last supper fell on which days. It is also important to note that the chapters (and the sections within the chapters) are not equal length, as it is not possible to treat this material equitably in terms of words. I apologize for this, as I like a book with even chapters, but the material simply defies equal sections. Some are far longer than others, largely as the text itself dictates.

I have hugely enjoyed the process of reflecting on these ideas, working up the material, reading the texts again and again and finally choosing what to put down on paper. I hope that you will also enjoy reading these passages and be inspired once more by the Jesus who set his face to Jerusalem and faithfully lived out his calling despite the cost.

Introduction

Twenty (or so) years on it is very difficult to call to mind the title of many of the undergraduate essays that I was set as a student. One, however, sticks in my mind and has accompanied me through many years of thinking, reflecting and praying: 'Why did Jesus die?' I must admit that the initial reason this question sticks in my mind is because it evokes (at least in me) a flippant response: 'Why did Jesus die?' Because not many people survived crucifixion.

Beyond flippancy, however, the question takes us right to the heart of our Christian faith and especially to the heart of our devotions during Holy Week. There are numerous serious answers that you can give to the question 'Why did Jesus die?' and during Holy Week we are driven back time and time again to asking that question in many different ways.

Christian tradition has provided many different answers to this one question. Some answers are more theological: he died that we might be forgiven; he died to redeem us from the power of sin; he died to reconcile us to God, and so on. The doctrine of the atonement significantly deals with the wide variety of theological answers given to the question of why Jesus died.

Other answers focus more on historical reasons for Jesus' death. Jesus died because his ministry put him in such conflict with either the Roman authorities or the Jewish leaders (or both) that his death became an inevitable outcome of this conflict. To this, some might add that the particular events of the last week of Jesus' life, including the fact that Jerusalem was packed with people coming for the feast of the Passover, meant that it was timing that led ultimately to his death. In other words if Jesus had come to Jerusalem having said and done exactly the same things a week later, he might not have died. It was surely the anxiety of the Romans about the crowds during Passover, combined with the concern of the Jewish leaders to avoid any unnecessary upheavals, that contributed to the inevitability of Jesus' death.

Circling around the many and varied answers to the question of why Jesus died is the deeply uncomfortable question of whether Jesus effectively committed suicide. Did he, knowing that his death would bring salvation, so manipulate timings and events that the only possible outcome was his own death?

Put crudely the question is, who or what was responsible for Jesus' death? God? The Romans? The Jews? Our sin? Jesus himself? The problem, of course, with crude questions is that they prompt crude answers, and crude answers rarely have much overlap with the truth. You only need to look at the horrific outcomes of anti-Semitism throughout Christian history to recognize that asking whether Jesus' death was the fault of the Jews (and then giving an affirmative answer) was a direct route towards some of the most evil actions of the previous century.

So crude questions and equally crude answers are to be avoided, but thoughtful, reflective questions and answers are not. The point seems to be that there is no one question, nor any one answer, that quite suffices. A range of factors – political, historical and theological – came together in the final week of Jesus' life in such a way as there could only be one outcome and we have been attempting ever since to mine the causes and consequences of this in order to discern the meaning(s) of the event.

In my view it is precisely the multiplicity of questions that need to be asked and the multiplicity of answers that can be given that brings us into the realm of truth: truth that points the finger of blame at no one person or group and that continues to open up perspectives rather than close them down.

The more I read the Gospels, the more convinced I am that the Gospel writers were also circling the same questions. The problem is that the way in which the Gospels are treated in liturgy and preaching means that their accounts are often harmonized so that their differences are smoothed out and harder to perceive. The result of this is that we often lose sight of the fact that each Gospel writer in his own way was asking the question why Jesus died and looking not only at what caused his death but what effect his death had on the world.

As a result, in this book we will be looking at the Gospel accounts as separately as possible. In particular we will be noting places where a Gospel writer has material not found elsewhere or has the same material in a different form and asking why this might be. We will look primarily at Matthew, Mark and Luke, because their accounts are closest together and easiest to read alongside each other, but from time to time where John's account is particularly important we will explore that too.

As in a number of my other books I would like to make clear that I am not a historical Jesus scholar and this book does not seek to prove (or disprove) the historicity of any of the events described in the Gospels. This is not my expertise and I shall leave it to others more qualified in this area than I to ruminate on the historicity of the events in question. My interest is in what the text says (rather than what we assume it says) and in why it might be saying it in a particular way. I aim for a close reading of the text in the original language (which I will explain when necessary) and to reflect on its meaning and significance.

My interest lies in what the Gospels tell us about who Jesus was. It lies in seeking to be inspired again by Jesus Christ, Son of God, who brought such transformative good news to the world. It lies in seeking to accompany him with heart, soul, mind and strength to his death and beyond. It lies in an encounter with the dying and rising Christ through the pages of Gospels and in trying to imagine what kind of life we might be able to live now as a consequence of all that Jesus was and did.

The journey to the empty tomb is of course Jesus' own journey but, if we accompany him with hearts on fire, minds alert and spirits open, then sometimes we will discover that it has also become our own journey, and that we too have been transformed by the God who raised Jesus from the dead.

1

Towards Jerusalem and the Temple

The Triumphal Entry

Matthew 21.1–11; Mark 11.1–10; Luke 19.29–40;
John 12.12–17

The account of Jesus' triumphal entry into Jerusalem marks the
moment when his death begins to look inevitable and unavoidable. Although the shadow of the cross has fallen over Jesus' life
and ministry for many chapters, his entry into Jerusalem is the
moment when the focus shifts significantly and we, the readers,
become aware that what follows will involve us in accompanying
Jesus to death and beyond.

Mark 11.1-10 When they were approaching Jerusalem, at Bethphage and Bethany, near the Mount of Olives, he sent two of his
disciples ²and said to them, 'Go into the village ahead of you, and
immediately as you enter it, you will find tied there a colt that has
never been ridden; untie it and bring it. ³If anyone says to you,
"Why are you doing this?" just say this, "The Lord needs it and
will send it back here immediately."' ⁴They went away and found
a colt tied near a door, outside in the street. As they were untying
it, ⁵some of the bystanders said to them, 'What are you doing,
untying the colt?' ⁶They told them what Jesus had said; and they
allowed them to take it.

> [7] Then they brought the colt to Jesus and threw their cloaks on it; and he sat on it. [8] Many people spread their cloaks on the road, and others spread leafy branches that they had cut in the fields. [9] Then those who went ahead and those who followed were shouting, 'Hosanna! Blessed is the one who comes in the name of the Lord! [10] Blessed is the coming kingdom of our ancestor David! Hosanna in the highest heaven!'

The popularly used title 'the triumphal entry' for this event is an intriguing one. As soon as you start thinking about it, it becomes clear that 'triumphal entry' can only be applied in the most ironic of senses to what happens to Jesus on his way into Jerusalem. Jesus is not triumphant at this point. His ministry is not complete. He has achieved only the most superficial recognition by the crowds and even his own disciples do not fully understand who he is. Even John's Gospel, which regards Jesus' death as his moment of glory, could not claim triumph as his death has not yet taken place.

So this is not in any usual sense a triumphal entry. It is an 'anti-triumph', or a triumph subverted. It is a triumph of the true nature of God: a nature that eschews pomp and splendour, a nature that acts out of love rather than status, and faithfulness rather than superficial gain. It is no surprise, therefore, that we cling to this title to describe this event, and rightly so, since it points us towards a subtle answer to the question, 'Why did Jesus die?' He died because God's understanding of what makes for a triumph is light years away from our own.

The prearrangement of the loan of a donkey

The account of the disciples going ahead to borrow a donkey is an intriguing one. It seems an unnecessary detail to insert and yet Matthew, Mark and Luke all include it. Only John resorts to saying that Jesus 'found' a donkey without exploring how or where he found it. One thing that this brief little snippet does for us is to remind us how little, in fact, we know of Jesus and his life. The implication of this story is that the donkey belongs to someone whom Jesus knows and with whom he has prearranged a loan of the donkey for the occasion. Who this person was, exactly how they knew Jesus or even how Jesus made such a prior arrangement, is lost in the mists of time.

What did Jesus' actions imply?

One of the questions that the triumphal entry raises is how much of the symbolic resonance of what was going on would have been picked up by the people at the time; the disciples then or afterwards; the first hearers of the stories; the Gospel writers and even the Gospel writers' audience. This passage is rich with symbolism and suggested meaning, but it is hard to know how much of this would have been recognized at the time, how much would have been suggested later by the way in which the tellers and writers of the story recounted the events, and how much has been read into the narrative by later interpreters. Nevertheless, it is worth taking time to stop and explore some of the richness implied in the text.

It is clear, when Jesus began to ride rather than walk, that something important was taking place. Perhaps this gives us something of a clue as to why Matthew, Mark and Luke all include the little story about the prearrangement of a loan of a donkey. This was a conscious, deliberate act, not an accidental one.

One donkey or two?

One of my favourite little moments of this story comes from Matthew's Gospel, where the disciples are sent to bring not one donkey but two: a mother and her foal:

> The disciples went and did as Jesus had directed them; they brought the donkey and the colt, and put their cloaks on them, and he sat on them. (21.6–7)

It is a moment where you can't help wondering what image was in Matthew's mind as he wrote. The reference to the donkey and the colt comes from Zechariah 9.9 (see below) which mentions both. Matthew's concern to show that this passage is being fulfilled here is so great that he includes both. It is much more likely that what was going on in Zechariah was Hebrew parallelism, where the same idea was repeated in a slightly different form for emphasis, but Matthew has taken it literally and included both animals in his narrative.

What he describes is hard to imagine. Does Jesus sit on both at once, or one after the other? The answer is probably that Matthew didn't picture anything; his concern was more to demonstrate the clear connection with Zechariah 9.9. Nevertheless, the odd notion of Jesus straddling two donkeys on his way into Jerusalem never fails to make me smile.

At this stage in his journey, the road to Jerusalem would have been thronged with people. Passover was a feast of obligation and so everyone in the country would, if at all possible, have converged in Jerusalem for the feast. This would have meant hundreds of thousands of people coming to the city. Many of these would have travelled together and friendships would have formed along the way. As a result, it would be possible to surmise that Jesus, tired from the long walk, had simply and coincidentally got on any old donkey belonging to one of the members of the crowd who were travelling that route together. But the explicit recounting of a specific journey made to collect a donkey for Jesus to ride removes any doubt in the matter. Jesus' riding of a donkey was no accidental, spur of the moment coincidence. It was deliberate and pre-planned. It is clear we are intended to read something into it, but what did it symbolize?

It is widely known that victorious Roman generals, when returning to Rome, would ride a white horse in their 'triumph'. A triumph was a carefully planned procession to show the people back in Rome what a great and marvellous general they were. In the procession they would bring all the loot (the treasures and the slaves) that they had purloined as a result of the victory and by doing so demonstrate how triumphant they were. If the notion of a Roman triumphal procession lies behind Jesus' entry into Jerusalem, it is clearly and importantly a subversion of this kind of event. The mode of transport is a donkey not a white horse; the people in the procession all came willingly and were not coerced; Jesus' triumph is yet to come and is in any case (as above) the kind of triumph only God would think triumphant.

So the narrative may bring to mind a Roman triumph, but much closer literary links can be found in Jewish tradition.

> **1 Maccabees 13.51** On the twenty-third day of the second month, in the one hundred and seventy-first year, the Jews entered it with praise and palm branches, and with harps and cymbals and stringed instruments, and with hymns and songs, because a great enemy had been crushed and removed from Israel.

One very striking passage from Maccabees recounts the victorious procession of the Maccabean army into Jerusalem after they had conquered Jerusalem in the Maccabean war against the Syrian Greek (Seleucid) Empire. Particularly striking here is the reference to the Maccabees being accompanied with praise and palm branches as Jesus also was. While the same objection applies to this as to the Roman triumph – that Jesus was not yet victorious – here it is possible that the actions of those accompanying Jesus into Jerusalem were intentional and hopeful. It could be that the crowd had this event from Maccabees in mind as they journeyed into Jerusalem and saw Jesus as a new Simon Maccabaeus come to drive a new occupying army out of their city.

Alongside this passage is also Zechariah, and if we connect the Maccabees with parts of Zechariah then Messianic bells begin to ring. There is, of course, Zechariah 9.9, which reminds us of the combined identity of the future king as both victorious and humble.

> **Zechariah 9.9** Rejoice greatly, O daughter Zion! Shout aloud, O daughter Jerusalem! Lo, your king comes to you; triumphant and victorious is he, humble and riding on a donkey, on a colt, the foal of a donkey.

This connection may also have resonances of 1 Kings 1.33 which described Solomon's journey to his coronation riding on a mule. But as well as this there is also Zechariah 14.4 which identifies the Mount of Olives as the place where the Lord will stand to begin the redemption of Israel.

> **Zechariah 14.4** On that day his feet shall stand on the Mount of Olives, which lies before Jerusalem on the east; and the Mount of Olives shall be split in two from east to west by a very wide valley ...

All of this implies that in Jesus' deliberate mounting of a donkey on the Mount of Olives were enough clues to suggest to the crowd that he was the longed-for king-like figure who had come to redeem his people, and that they responded by hailing him as the crowd had done to Simon Maccabaeus only 150 or so years before. It's intriguing to ask what happened to the crowd following Jesus' entry into Jerusalem; they appear simply to melt away as the narrative turns once more to Jesus and his followers, but why? What was it that so gripped their attention one minute and so entirely slipped from their minds the next? What is likely is that when Jesus did nothing more dramatic, more pressing needs (finding somewhere to stay, locating family members, and so on) took over and their adulation of Jesus took second place in their minds.

Cry 'Hosanna'

For many people it comes as quite a surprise to discover that the word 'Hosanna' comes, in English, only here in the Bible; though in Hebrew it appears here and in Psalm 118.25. 'Hosanna' is so widely used in worship songs and in hymns that it is easy to assume that it is dotted throughout the psalms with as much abandon as the word 'Hallelujah'. It is not, and in English translations is found only in Matthew, Mark and John's versions of this account. Luke, as he does elsewhere, removes the need for including Hebrew words by omitting the phrase.

Matthew 21.9	Mark 11.9–10	Luke 19.38	John 12.13
'Hosanna to the Son of David! Blessed is the one who comes in the name of the Lord! Hosanna in the highest heaven!'	'Hosanna! Blessed is the one who comes in the name of the Lord! [10]Blessed is the coming kingdom of our ancestor David! Hosanna in the highest heaven!'	'Blessed is the king who comes in the name of the Lord! Peace in heaven, and glory in the highest heaven!'	'Hosanna! Blessed is the one who comes in the name of the Lord – the King of Israel!'

If we compare this to its original form in Psalm 118.25–26, some interesting points emerge.

> **Psalm 118.25–26** Save us, we beseech you, O Lord! O Lord, we beseech you, give us success! [26]Blessed is the one who comes in the name of the Lord. We bless you from the house of the Lord.

The first and most obvious point is that 'Hosanna' is not present in the English translation of the psalm. This is for a good reason. It is a Hebrew word and all other Hebrew words in the Old Testament are translated, so this was as well. In the Gospels, however, the Hebrew word is inserted into the middle of sentences that are otherwise all in Greek and so, to draw readers' attention to this, the English translators of the text have kept it in its original Hebrew. This, of course, raises the question of why the Gospel writers kept one word from Psalm 118.25–26 in Hebrew and translated the rest. The answer seems to be that the word 'Hosanna' had become important in its own right (see the reference to shouting 'Hosanna' at the Feast of the Tabernacles in the text box below), and therefore its use here is of more importance than simply quoting the psalms in Hebrew.

Cloaks

The closest parallel to spreading cloaks on the ground can be found in 2 Kings 9.13, when, after Jehu was anointed with oil, the crowd spread their cloaks on the ground and hailed him as king.

Leafy branches

Some scholars have drawn a connection between this event and the Feast of the Tabernacles. At that feast it was customary to wave palm branches whenever the word 'Hosanna' from Psalm 118.25 was mentioned. This connection is unlikely, given the importance of these events being clustered around Passover but the resonances are, nevertheless, very interesting and have led some scholars to question whether the entry into Jerusalem

> really took place during Tabernacles not Passover (a view that unsurprisingly has not received overwhelming support).

It is also interesting to notice the subtle shifting of meaning in the word from its original usage, to its use in the Gospels and then to its common usage today. *Hoshi'a na* means literally 'save now', and in its context in Psalm 118 is a cry of supplication by the whole people of God that God would hear them and save them. The word's usage in the Gospels suggests that this has shifted from being simply a prayer to something closer to a statement of confidence. In much modern use it has become such a statement of confidence that in some contexts it feels like a cry of praise akin to Hallelujah.

This shift in meaning can probably be ascribed to the popularity of Psalm 118 around the time of Jesus as a psalm expressing the future hope of Israel's coming salvation by a future Davidic king-like figure. In Rabbinic literature (for example, *Babylonian Talmud Pesachim* 119a), Psalm 118.25ff was used with particular reference to such a figure who would come to redeem Israel, so this might lie in the background of its use here.

It is also worth noting that none of the quotations in the Gospels is exact. Matthew and Mark double the use of 'Hosanna' and also insert an overt Davidic reference which is only at best implicit in Psalm 118. Luke's insertion is particularly interesting as it echoes the song of the angels in Luke 2.14.

> **Luke 19.38** 'Blessed is the king who comes in the name of the Lord! Peace in heaven, and glory in the highest heaven!'

The key difference, though, is that in Luke 2.14 peace is said to be on earth whereas here peace is only in heaven. The crowds mimicking of the song of the angels makes them in Luke's Gospel proclaimers, like the angels, of the in-breaking of God's kingdom on earth. However we are now at the stage in Luke's narrative where time and time again he stresses the future catastrophic fate that the people have set for themselves, from which the only conclusion can be that peace is not to be found on earth, at least not yet.

The challenge of the chanting of Psalm 118 is that although it was particularly associated with the Feast of the Tabernacles, it was more generally associated, along with all the other Hallel psalms in 113–118, as a psalm of ascent, or a psalm sung on the way to a major festival in Jerusalem. The question that lingers then is how much significance we should place on its being sung here, if it would have been sung anyway. The answer seems to be that significance is to be found not in any one thing but in the con-fluence of events: Jesus suddenly and deliberately riding a donkey, this taking place on the Mount of Olives, the spreading of the cloaks to welcome a king and the singing of a well-loved psalm that looked forward to a king-figure like David coming to redeem Israel. This confluence of events is so deeply and richly suggestive of meaning to someone living in the first century that it is no won-der that the people around Jesus began to draw conclusions about who Jesus was – even if these conclusions did not cause them to continue following him after his entry into Jerusalem.

* * *

Reflection

The events that took place on what we now call Palm Sunday all raise the question of what it is that makes or helps us to recog-nize who Jesus really is. On that day Jesus was the same person that he had been for the rest of his ministry. So what was it that made the crowd begin to recognize and proclaim his Messianic significance? The donkey on the Mount of Olives might have been enough but I can't help wondering whether, as I suggest above, that it was the bringing together of a number of strands that began to make the penny drop. Could it be that the singing of Psalm 118, as was customary on the way to a major festival, while Jesus was on a donkey, on the Mount of Olives, on the way into Jerusalem, brought Jesus' identity into focus in a new way?

Having said that, we must not make too much of this new realization: Jesus arrived in Jerusalem and the crowd melted away. The human attention span is very poor indeed. Often today we blame the speed of our society, technology in general and mobile phones in particular for shortening our attention span, but the Gospel narratives suggest it was ever thus. Even at a time when there were few external factors to distract, the arrival into Jerusalem, the need to find somewhere to stay and something to eat seems to have been sufficient to pull people away from their dawning realization that the one they had accompanied into Jerusalem waving palms and with shouts of 'Hosanna' might just have been the one for whom they had waited for so long. The Gospel writers give little explanation about why the crowd disappeared and perhaps this is simply because it needed little explanation. Even when faced with the most important news of all, it is far too easy to be distracted and for our attention to fade.

All of this is important to bear in mind as we seek to live out our Christian life. Why is it that sometimes we put our heart and soul into explaining the mysteries of Christian truth, or of proclaiming Jesus, and people simply do not grasp what we are talking about? The answer may be that the recognition of truth requires more than one factor and that we need to keep on speaking, proclaiming and acting in the hope that one day the right confluence of factors will help people to grasp what we are talking about. It may also be that action rich with meaning (like Jesus' riding a donkey on the Mount of Olives) can speak far more loudly than words, and perhaps we need to pay as much attention to what we do and how we do it as to what we say.

Alongside this we need to recognize that all human nature is fickle, and that we cannot always process or stay with a dawning realization of truth. If the crowd could not even linger in Jerusalem with Jesus for a day or two after shouting 'Hosanna' and waving palms no wonder we also struggle to stay with and live out our recognition of who Jesus really is when we encounter him in our lives. This doesn't mean that we shouldn't try but it does offer us a level of forgiveness when we fail.

11

The Cursing of the Fig Tree, the Cleansing of the Temple and the Parable of the Tenants

Matthew 21.12–43; Mark 11.11—12.12

If the number of emails I receive from panic-stricken preachers in the week before this passage is set in the lectionary is anything to go by, one of the passages that seems to strike some of the greatest terror into preachers' hearts is the passage of the Cursing of the Fig Tree in Mark. Many difficult passages in the Gospels are just that, difficult passages, and as a New Testament expert I can do little more than sympathize with the lot of having to preach on said passage and offer a few hints that might help people get into it better. This much-feared passage, however, is not all that difficult when you read it in its context and appreciate what is going on beneath the narrative in Mark's Gospel.

> **Mark 11.11–25 and 12.1–12**   Then he entered Jerusalem and went into the temple; and when he had looked around at everything, as it was already late, he went out to Bethany with the twelve.
>
> [12]On the following day, when they came from Bethany, he was hungry. [13]Seeing in the distance a fig tree in leaf, he went to see whether perhaps he would find anything on it. When he came to it, he found nothing but leaves, for it was not the season for figs. [14]He said to it, 'May no one ever eat fruit from you again.' And his disciples heard it.
>
> [15]Then they came to Jerusalem. And he entered the temple and began to drive out those who were selling and those who were buying in the temple, and he overturned the tables of the money-changers and the seats of those who sold doves; [16]and he would not allow anyone to carry anything through the temple. [17]He was teaching and saying, 'Is it not written,
>
> "My house shall be called a house of prayer for all the nations"?
> But you have made it a den of robbers.'

[18]And when the chief priests and the scribes heard it, they kept looking for a way to kill him; for they were afraid of him, because the whole crowd was spellbound by his teaching. [19]And when evening came, Jesus and his disciples went out of the city.

[20]In the morning as they passed by, they saw the fig tree withered away to its roots. [21]Then Peter remembered and said to him, 'Rabbi, look! The fig tree that you cursed has withered.' [22]Jesus answered them, 'Have faith in God. [23]Truly I tell you, if you say to this mountain, "Be taken up and thrown into the sea", and if you do not doubt in your heart, but believe that what you say will come to pass, it will be done for you. [24]So I tell you, whatever you ask for in prayer, believe that you have received it, and it will be yours.

[25]Whenever you stand praying, forgive, if you have anything against anyone; so that your Father in heaven may also forgive you your trespasses.'

12.1–12 Then he began to speak to them in parables. 'A man planted a vineyard, put a fence around it, dug a pit for the wine press, and built a watchtower; then he leased it to tenants and went to another country. [2]When the season came, he sent a slave to the tenants to collect from them his share of the produce of the vineyard. [3]But they seized him, and beat him, and sent him away empty-handed. [4]And again he sent another slave to them; this one they beat over the head and insulted. [5]Then he sent another, and that one they killed. And so it was with many others; some they beat, and others they killed. [6]He had still one other, a beloved son. Finally he sent him to them, saying, "They will respect my son." [7]But those tenants said to one another, "This is the heir; come, let us kill him, and the inheritance will be ours." [8]So they seized him, killed him, and threw him out of the vineyard. [9]What then will the owner of the vineyard do? He will come and destroy the tenants and give the vineyard to others. [10]Have you not read this scripture:

> "The stone that the builders rejected
> has become the cornerstone;
> ¹¹this was the Lord's doing,
> and it is amazing in our eyes"?'
> ¹² When they realized that he had told this parable against them,
> they wanted to arrest him, but they feared the crowd. So they left
> him and went away.

Psalm 118 in Mark's account

In order for it to make sense you need to do two things:

- Read the whole sweep of the passage including the triumphal entry into Jerusalem and the Parable of the Tenants.
- Recognize the importance of Psalm 118 behind Mark's narrative.

Although Psalm 118 is used in all the Gospels in some form or another at this point, it is in Mark's Gospel that it is stitched carefully and thoughtfully into a large sweep of the narrative. This begins at the triumphal entry with the quotation from Psalm 118.25.

> **Mark 11.9–10**
> 'Hosanna!
> Blessed is the one who comes in the name of the Lord!
> ¹⁰ Blessed is the coming kingdom of our ancestor David!
> Hosanna in the highest heaven!'

And reaches its climax in the Parable of the Tenants, in which is a quotation from Psalm 118.22.

> **Mark 12.10-11** 'The stone that the builders rejected has become the cornerstone;
> [11]this was the Lord's doing, and it is amazing in our eyes.'

The presence of two apparently unconnected verses from the same psalm may appear to provide underwhelming proof of connection until you reflect upon the context in which they are placed.

Psalm 118 records the victory of a king, probably a Davidic king, returning from battle. It is set in the context of a song of praise for victory which the people greeting the returning king are to pick up and join in with. Verses 1–18 describe the battle and the way that God intervened to bring about victory.

> **Psalm 118.19-29**
> Open to me the gates of righteousness,
>   that I may enter through them
>   and give thanks to the Lord.
> [20]This is the gate of the Lord;
>   the righteous shall enter through it.
> [21]I thank you that you have answered me
>   and have become my salvation.
> [22]The stone that the builders rejected
>   has become the chief cornerstone.
> [23]This is the Lord's doing;
>   it is marvellous in our eyes.
> [24]This is the day that the Lord has made;
>   let us rejoice and be glad in it.
> [25]Save us, we beseech you, O Lord!
>   O Lord, we beseech you, give us success!
> [26]Blessed is the one who comes in the name of the Lord.
>   We bless you from the house of the Lord.
> [27]The Lord is God,
>   and he has given us light.
> Bind the festal procession with branches,
>   up to the horns of the altar.

> [28]You are my God, and I will give thanks to you;
>   you are my God, I will extol you.
> [29]O give thanks to the Lord, for he is good,
>   for his steadfast love endures for ever.

Many scholars agree that verses 19 to the end recount the king's arrival at the temple gates (19), a response by the gatekeepers to remind him and others that these are the gates of righteousness (20), a personal thanksgiving by the king for salvation (21), the testimony of the accompanying people that they recognize what God has done (22–25), and then a response by the priests of the temple who bless the one who has come in the name of the Lord and lead him in celebrating his victory (26–27), followed by more thanksgiving (28–29).

What is important for our story in the Gospels is that verses 25 'Hosanna' and 26 'Blessed is the one who comes in the name of the Lord' are a conversation between the crowd who accompany the king and the priests in the temple. In other words the crowd beg God for salvation ('Save us we beseech you, O Lord') and the priests respond with a recognition of who the king is and an assurance God has blessed him.

In stark contrast, in the Gospels, the crowd sing both parts (the plea for salvation and the blessing), because the temple authorities are at first absolutely silent and then look for a way to kill Jesus. There is no recognition or blessing of Jesus from the temple in Mark. This reaches its climax in Mark 11.27—12.12 when Jesus enters into direct conflict with the chief priests, the scribes and the elders and they decide that he must die.

Mark stresses the absence of their blessing from Jesus' triumphal entry by having Jesus going directly to the temple after entering Jerusalem. The cries of 'Hosanna' on the way are the perfect cue for the priests to respond as they do in Psalm 118, but instead there is an eerie silence. Luke highlights the absence in a different way by having the Pharisees (who though not priests symbolize for Luke Jewish authority) ask Jesus to shut his disciples up.

It is here that the significance of the fig tree comes to the fore and Mark makes sure we see its significance by wrapping the narrative about the fig tree around the story of the Cleansing of the Temple and then Jesus' conversation with the chief priests, scribes and elders. In Mark the order goes:

- The triumphal entry (Mark 11.1–10).
- Jesus went to the temple but was not welcomed by the priests and went to Bethany again (11.11).
- Jesus returned to Jerusalem and on the way cursed the fig tree (11.12–14).
- Jesus 'cleansed' the temple (11.15–19).
- The next morning they see that the fig tree has withered (11.20–25).
- Jesus converses with the chief priests and ends up telling the Parable of the Tenants.

In the Old Testament, fig trees symbolize God's blessing and abundance. Regular reference is made throughout the Old Testament to lack of figs on the fig trees as a symbol of Israel's spiritual barrenness.

> **Jeremiah 8.13** When I wanted to gather them, says the Lord, there are no grapes on the vine, nor figs on the fig tree; even the leaves are withered, and what I gave them has passed away from them.

And conversely to the longed-for future when everyone could eat from their own vine and fig tree and would have so much that they would be able to share it with others.

> **Zechariah 3.10** On that day, says the Lord of hosts, you shall invite each other to come under your vine and fig tree.

As a result fruitful fig trees – like vineyards – symbolized the glorious future that God had in store for his people, but fig trees with no fruit are of little use to anyone. Even more importantly fig trees have the next season's fruit on them even when they are not in fruiting season, so a fig tree without any fruit on it at all is not going to fruit in either the short or the long term. In wrapping this story around the Cleansing of the Temple, Mark is showing us how to understand what Jesus did in the temple.

The Cursing of the Temple and the Fig Tree

The Cleansing of the Temple has long caused heated discussion among scholars. The popular interpretation of Jesus' action is that he objected to the merchants changing money and selling animals in the temple precincts. The problem is that the whole temple cult relied on this. Temple tax was paid in shekels not denarii (the Roman coinage) so the people of Israel needed to change their money in order to pay the tax. The simplest place to do this was the temple itself. In addition to this, the sacrificial system in the temple required the animals that people wished to offer for sacrifice to have been checked for purity by temple officials and to be 'without blemish' (see Exodus 12.5; Leviticus 1.3). In his defence of Judaism, *Against Apion* 2.108, Josephus indicated that there were 20,000 priests in Israel in the first century. Even if this number is an over-exaggeration, there was a large number of priests in this period. At a major festival such as Passover they would all have been on duty. If you extrapolate outwards from the number of priests to how many sacrifices they would have done, then not only does the temple become very smelly and very messy, but also very busy. The only realistic way of sacrificing this many animals was to pre-certify the animals as clean. The animal traders in the temple were simply selling the pre-certified animals to the worshippers.

Given this, Jesus' action may well have been more symbolic in intention. It was probably not designed to criticize the money-changers or animal traders but to be, in fact, a more far-reaching critique of the whole temple system. This seems to be confirmed by the fact that his 'cleansing' did not appear to disrupt the temple worship much: the woman paying her temple tax in Mark 12.41–44 remained able to do so only a short time later and the Passover also went ahead unaffected.

This interpretation is also supported by the subsequent telling of the Parable of the Tenants which in its turn critiqued the chief priests, the scribes and the elders. The point of that parable is that the tenants did not do what they were meant to do: they were meant to guard and tend their master's asset and then deliver to him the profits when he asked for them. Instead they attempted to keep first the profits and then the whole vineyard for themselves. In the same way the fig tree did not do what it was meant to: produce fruit. It neither had fruit about to ripen nor any for the next season either.

Absentee landlords

The Parable of the Tenants makes more sense when you recognize the prevalence of absentee landlords particularly in Galilee. Although the law forbade inequity and the unfair accumulation of land, by the time of the first century there were a large number of landowners who owned significant tracts of land. Many owned high-quality farming land but lived in Jerusalem. The people to whom Jesus was speaking in this parable were quite probably absentee landlords themselves, so the parable would have had been even more hard-hitting.

This leads to the conclusion that Jesus' problem with the temple was not sacrifice, the changing of money nor indeed the selling of animals but, like the tenants in the vineyard and the fig tree, it was not doing what it was meant to do. The temple was meant to be the gateway to heaven, to be the place where God could be present on earth. As such it should have been the place where God's son, the longed-for king-figure like David, was recognized, welcomed and blessed (as the king was in Psalm 118). But, not only did the priests not bless Jesus on his arrival into Jerusalem, they also sought ways to kill him.

The quotation Jesus cites seems to support this: 'He was teaching and saying, "Is it not written, 'My house shall be called a house of prayer for all the nations'? But you have made it a den of robbers"' (Mark 11.17). The first half of the quotation is drawn from Isaiah 56.6–8.

Isaiah 56.6–8

And the foreigners who join themselves to the Lord,

to minister to him, to love the name of the Lord, and to be his servants,

all who keep the sabbath, and do not profane it, and hold fast my covenant—

[7]these I will bring to my holy mountain, and make them joyful in my house of prayer;

their burnt offerings and their sacrifices will be accepted on my altar;

for my house shall be called a house of prayer for all peoples.

[8]Thus says the Lord God, who gathers the outcasts of Israel,

I will gather others to them besides those already gathered.

This passage looks forward to the role the temple will play on 'the day of the Lord' when God will intervene to save his people. On that day people from all nations of the world will stream to the temple and be joyful in God's house of prayer. Instead of this the temple of Jesus' day excluded and rejected people – even Jesus who had come to save God's people – and become instead a den of robbers, as the temple is called in Jeremiah.

Jeremiah 7.11 Has this house, which is called by my name, become a den of robbers in your sight? You know, I too am watching, says the Lord.

Mark deliberately emphasizes this by his choice of the Greek word, *lēstēs*. This means more than just a thief and instead refers to a politically motivated outlaw whose goal was to overthrow the current system. Jesus' accusation that the temple had become a den of outlaws implies that he is claiming that those ruling the temple are seeking power for themselves and by so doing are overthrowing God's power. They have, effectively, stolen the temple and are using it for their own political gain. In short, the temple was not doing what it ought to have done and Jesus' action cursed it, just like he cursed the fig tree.

The Cleansing of the Temple in John (John 2.13–22)

The account of the Cleansing of the Temple in John's Gospel is noteworthy for two main reasons. The first is, of course, because it is much, much earlier in the chronology of the narrative. In John, Jesus cleanses the temple as one of the first things he does in his ministry. Although some scholars have argued that Jesus cleansed the temple twice, once at the start of his ministry and once at the end, few are persuaded by this as a theory. Much more likely, given the way John writes, is that he has put the event at the start of Jesus' ministry for a particular reason. You do not have to read far in John before you realize that, more than in any other Gospel, its whole focus is the cross and the coming of the 'hour' in which Jesus will be glorified. Theming the Gospel with three Passover festivals and putting the Cleansing of the Temple at the start serves to remind us of this focus. It also means that Jesus provokes the Jewish authorities to anger also at the beginning and this opposition hangs over the rest of the Gospel.

Second, the account in John is much more detailed than in the other Gospels. In Matthew, Mark and Luke mention is only made of the selling of doves; John also mentions cattle and sheep. John gives the vivid image of Jesus spilling the coins and driving out the traders with a whip. The words used by Jesus are also different. Here the reference is to Zechariah 14.21: 'And there shall no longer be traders in the house of the Lord of hosts

---

on that day.' This puts the focus of John's telling of the event much more on the end times, when trading is no longer needed because God will be present among his people in a new way.

As a result, the meaning of the event changes in John and picks up the themes of John's prologue. Now the Word made flesh is present in the midst of the people, there is no more need for the temple to function as it always has. In John, then, the cleansing is a sign of the end times proclaimed by the Word made flesh and living among us.

In Mark's Gospel, I would suggest that we might be better to call this whole incident 'The Cursing of the Fig Tree and the Temple' since that then draws our attention to the whole event. What is important is that after the cursing, the fig tree withered and died. Jesus' action in the temple, then, was more than 'just' a criticism; it has the suggestion of a prophetic action. Just as the fig tree withered and died, so too would the temple: and, of course, we now know that it did in AD 70. Mark's Gospel suggests the roots of that destruction could be found 40 years or so earlier in Jesus' actions in the temple.

Matthew's Fig Tree (Matthew 21.18–22)

Matthew's version of the Cursing of the Fig Tree changes its meaning quite significantly. In Matthew the whole event takes place after the Cleansing of the Temple and the fig tree withered immediately. As a result, in Matthew, the whole episode becomes much more about the power of faith and prayer than about the cursing of the temple.

This short account offers a fascinating vignette on the Gospel writers' art. Whenever we recount things we have to make constant decisions about where to place emphasis and what each event means. The Gospel writers were constantly faced with this question. What fascinates me is those occasions when they have clearly come to different decisions on the importance of an event.

In my view the fig tree is one of those occasions. Mark sees the event as an overarching way of interpreting what Jesus did in the temple; whereas Matthew sees the event in a more focused way about prayer and its power.

Reading the Cleansing of the Temple like this, ties the event much more closely to the 'apocalyptic' chapters of Mark 13, Matthew 24 and Luke 21 which talk in such vivid language about a cataclysm to come. It can be tempting to read these chapters as an odd insertion into the last week of Jesus' life with little connection to the other events mentioned in surrounding chapters, but if this reading of the Cleansing of the Temple is correct then the apocalyptic chapters fit fully and properly into this last week of Jesus' life. The cataclysm of Jesus' death is approaching but the events do not end there. The ripples of what is about to happen will continue to spread and to affect the world long after Jesus' death and resurrection, not only at the destruction of the temple 40 years later but onwards from there to the end times. There is insufficient space in this book to tackle the 'apocalyptic' chapters and the extensive scholarly discussions that have taken place about what these chapters refer to (the future end or the destruction of the temple, or a mixture of both). In some ways it is a shame that these chapters are transferred in people's minds to Advent rather than Holy Week because it removes them from the last week of Jesus' life and their close intermingling with Jesus' approaching death. In terms of devotion within the churches, however, Advent is where they are to be found and so will not be explored in detail here. Nevertheless it is worth being aware of the way in which Jesus' actions and interactions during this week time and time again focus the attention onto a future beyond his death and resurrection.

* * *

Reflection

The Cursing of the Temple and the Fig Tree remind us power-fully of the profound importance of institutions living up to their calling. The temple officials had excellent reasons for failing to ensure that the temple was 'a house of prayer for all nations'. They lived day to day attempting simply to survive. Life with an occupying Roman army was precarious at the best of times and an occasion when the city was full to bursting with pilgrims for a major festival was not the best of times. The chief priests' task was not an enviable one. The Romans held them to account for what went on. It is hardly surprising that they were unable to recognize and welcome the presence of Jesus, the Messiah, Son of God, in their midst.

It may be understandable why leaders of the people were unable to welcome Jesus for who he really was, but they failed to do so and Jesus' action in the temple condemned this failure. This brings us to reflect on our own institutional failures: under-standable they may be but failures they remain. Our churches do not quite face the same challenge as the temple did, since the advent of Jesus means that God can be encountered in many different places and contexts; nevertheless we are still called to draw people to God and where we fail to do that we should take this failure seriously and ask for forgiveness.

Our vocations, however, are not just corporate and institu-tional but also personal and individual. Each one of us is called to live up to our calling and to be who God calls us to be. The fig tree's vocation was straightforward and easy to discern: it should produce fruit. The question for each one of us is – What is our vocation? What is our equivalent of producing fruit? And are we confident that we will be fruiting in both the short and the long term? While the answer to these questions will be dif-ferent for each one of us, there is a strand to vocation that affects us all. The temple officials' major failure was their inability to recognize, proclaim, welcome and bless God when he appeared in their midst. Much of Jesus' teaching in the week following these events in the temple focuses around discernment and recognition.

The most obvious place is slightly later on in Mark 13.28–29 where we find another fig tree; the Parable of the Fig Tree. As Jesus observes, when the fig tree gets leaves everyone knows how to read what these leaves mean: that summer was coming. Jesus' followers needed to become equally astute readers of the signs of the kingdom. This remains as true now as it ever was. We should all be people who strain with every fibre of our being to recognize God and the actions of God whenever and wherever they break into our world – even when that in-breaking takes the most unexpected and least desired of forms.

Between the Cleansing of the Temple and the Last Supper

Mark 12.13—14.9; Matthew 21.14—26.13; Luke 19.41—21.38

Between the Cleansing of the Temple and the preparations for the last supper we find in Matthew, Mark and Luke a range of conversations and responses to Jesus. There are far too many to do them all justice but it is worth noting the sweep of events included in each Gospel (since although some details differ the major foci remain the same). It is also worth picking out a few key passages which illustrate the whole.

Matthew		Mark		Luke	
21.23–27	Questioning of Jesus' authority by chief priests and elders.	11.27–31	Questioning of Jesus' authority by chief priests and elders.	20.1–8	Questioning of Jesus' authority by chief priests and scribes.
21.28–32	Parable of the Two Sons.				
21.33–46	Parable of the Tenants.	12.1–12	Parable of the Tenants.	20.9–19	Parable of the Tenants.
22.1–14	Parable of the Wedding Banquet.				
22.15–22	Question about tax.	12.13–17	Question about tax.	20.21–26	Question about tax.
22.23–33	Question about resurrection.	12.18–27	Question about resurrection.	20.27–39	Question about resurrection.
22.34–40	Question about the law.	12.28–34	Question about the law.		
22.41–43	Jesus asks a question about the Messiah.	12.35–37	Jesus asks a question about the Messiah.	20.40–45	Jesus asks a question about the Messiah.
23.1–36	Woes to scribes and Pharisees.	12.37–40	Beware the scribes.	20.46–47	Beware the scribes.

Matthew		Mark		Luke	
		12.41–44	Widow's mite.	21.1–4	Widow's mite.
23.37–39	Jesus laments over Jerusalem.			19.41–44	Jesus laments over Jerusalem.
24.1–51	Signs of the end.	13.1–37	Signs of the end.	21.5–38	Signs of the end.
25.1–13	Parable of the Bridesmaids.				
25.14–30	Parable of the Talents.				
25.31–46	Parable of the Sheep and the Goats.				
26.1–5	Leaders conspire to kill Jesus.	14.1–2	Leaders conspire to kill Jesus.	22.1–2	Leaders conspire to kill Jesus.
26.6–13	Anointing of Jesus' feet.	14.3–9	Anointing of Jesus' feet.		
26.14–16	Judas' decision to betray Jesus.	14.10–11	Judas' decision to betray Jesus.	22.3–7	Judas' decision to betray Jesus.

While tables can be dull and hard to read, the value of one like this is that it helps us to see at a glance what is going on in the telling of the story in each of the Gospels. When laid out like this it is easy to see that although Matthew's Gospel contains many more stories than the other Gospels, these are stories of a very similar kind to the ones already in Mark and Luke. The focus of this material in all the Gospels is on Jesus' increasing conflict with the Jewish authorities. They came to him and asked challenging questions about authority, about tax, about resurrection and about the law. He in his turn defeated their questioning time and time again, challenging them about their attitude to the Messiah and turning the attention of the disciples to the future and the signs of the end.

When you realize this it becomes clear that the additional material in Matthew's Gospel contributes simply a few more examples of a similar type of teaching.

There are two blocks of additional parables in Matthew. The first block of parables in chapter 21 contains additional reflections on who is worthy to inherit the kingdom and the second block of parables in chapter 25 keeps the focus of chapter 24 a little longer in offering reflections on what we should do while waiting for the end. All in all, whether in Matthew's longer account or Mark and Luke's shorter ones the overall impression of this material is of ever-increasing conflict between Jesus and the Jewish authorities, a conflict that can have only one outcome.

In the midst of this conflict, three small stories stand out and are worthy of further reflection.

The Widow's Gift

Mark 12.41–44; Luke 21.1–4

> **Mark 12.41-44** He sat down opposite the treasury, and watched the crowd putting money into the treasury. Many rich people put in large sums. [42]A poor widow came and put in two small copper coins, which are worth a penny. [43]Then he called his disciples and said to them, 'Truly I tell you, this poor widow has put in more than all those who are contributing to the treasury. [44]For all of them have contributed out of their abundance; but she out of her poverty has put in everything she had, all she had to live on.'

The well-known and well-loved story of the Widow's Gift is not in Matthew's Gospel but is in Mark and Luke. It is not hard to work out why this is. The widow in Mark and Luke symbolizes a person whose attitude to God is right. Unlike the scribes mentioned in the previous passage, this widow was not seeking her own glory or exploiting others for her own benefit, but instead responded to the generosity of God out of the little that she had with a generosity of her own. Matthew has less need for such a story since he had already included the Parables of the Two Sons and the Wedding Banquet, alongside the Parable of the Tenants as further reflections on the question of who was worthy to inherit the kingdom of God. Those parables play a similar role to this story as both imply, either directly or indirectly, that those who inherit the kingdom do so on the grounds of their own actions and readiness not their status.

The generosity of the woman is stressed in both Gospels by the fact that she threw in two coins. Someone who had very little could have been forgiven for contributing a single coin – the use of two coins implies that she gave the most that she could. The word used for these coins is *leptos*. This was the smallest, thinnest and lowest denomination of all the Roman coins. Using this coinage the least the woman could have given would have been one *leptos*, hence the implication of her generosity.

Temple tax and gifts

An important point to notice is that the woman was not paying temple tax. Temple tax was paid by all men 20 years old and above, using a particular coin, a near pure-silver half-shekel coin, minted in Palestine but known as Tyrian shekels (because they had been minted in Tyre until around 18 BC). These coins were only used for the temple tax and for nothing else, hence the need for the money-changers in the temple to change money from Roman coinage used every day to the coin used for temple tax.

Temple tax was one half-shekel per year and was used for the day-to-day running of the temple, for example the sacrifices and libations. Gifts were also encouraged for the temple's upkeep.

We know that the widow was not paying temple tax for two reasons: first because she was a woman and women did not pay temple tax and second because two *lepta* would have been far too small an amount to pay. Instead she was making a free-will offering or gift for the upkeep of the temple (which could be

---

done in Roman coinage). This only emphasizes the generosity of her act.

It is probably worth adding that the description of the money given to Judas after he betrayed Jesus suggests that he was paid in Tyrian shekels, that is, temple tax money. There is surely an irony that money given for the day-to-day upkeep of the temple was used to ensure the death of Jesus.

Jesus' Lament over Jerusalem

Matthew 23.37–39; Luke 19.41–44

One important part of this final week is Jesus' lament over the city in Matthew and Luke. In Matthew's Gospel, Jesus' lament took place after he had pronounced woes over the scribes and Pharisees; in Luke's Gospel a similar event took place during the triumphal entry.

Matthew 23.37–39	Luke 19.41–44
'Jerusalem, Jerusalem, the city that kills the prophets and stones those who are sent to it! How often have I desired to gather your children together as a hen gathers her brood under her wings, and you were not willing! 38See, your house is left to you, desolate. 39For I tell you, you will not see me again until you say, "Blessed is the one who comes in the name of the Lord."'	As he came near and saw the city, he wept over it, 42saying, 'If you, even you, had only recognized on this day the things that make for peace! But now they are hidden from your eyes. 43Indeed, the days will come upon you, when your enemies will set up ramparts around you and surround you, and hem you in on every side. 44They will crush you to the ground, you and your children within you, and they will not leave within you one stone upon another; because you did not recognize the time of your visitation from God.'

Although the wording of these two accounts is very different, the sentiment is similar. At times in this narrative we could be forgiven for concluding that Jesus was in deliberate conflict with Jerusalem and its leaders and that he relished the conflict that was to come. Each of these passages brings home powerfully the level of regret and pain that Jesus felt at the inevitability of what was to happen.

In Matthew's Gospel, the lament seems to pick up the theme of the Parable of the Tenants again: Jesus yearned to gather the whole city together and to keep it safe, but the authorities refused to let go of their grip on the city (just as the tenants did in the parable). In 23.38 Jesus says that they will get what they want but will discover that it wasn't what they had in mind. As is so often the case, grasping something with a strong grip squeezes the life out of what we wanted to cling on to so that it is no longer the glittering prize it used to be.

Desolate: the word translated 'desolate' in the NRSV (23.38) is, in Greek, the word for 'wilderness' (the same word is used to describe the place that Jesus went to for temptation in Matthew 4). In other words the authorities will get what they want – sole ownership of the city but they will discover it has turned into a desert.

A similar scene in Luke's Gospel occurs before any of the major conflict of the last week of Jesus' life has taken place at all. Here Luke begins to probe a theme that runs importantly through the whole of this last week of Jesus' life. Luke probably more than any of the other Gospels keeps our eyes focused not only on the catastrophe of Jesus' death but also on the destruction that is coming to Jerusalem as a whole in AD 70. This catastrophe he traces back directly to Jerusalem's failure to recognize Jesus when they could. The implication of what Jesus says here is that the fall of the temple might have been avoided had they been able to recognize who Jesus was and what difference he made in the world.

> **Visitation:** The word translated visitation in Luke is the Greek word *episcope*. God's 'oversight' of the people was the opportunity to recognize Jesus for who he really was. Their failure to do so brought judgement on them, a judgement the effects of which were felt 40 years later.

Matthew's account of Jesus' lament ends with its vision fixed entirely on the future. We noted at the triumphal entry that those who should have been welcoming the coming king from the temple were at best eerily silent. Matthew 23.39 picks up this theme once more. They will see Jesus again (we are left to assume that it will be when the Son of Man comes on the clouds of glory) and then, when they do, they will recognize him for who he is and say the words that were so absent the first time.

The Anointing of Jesus

Matthew 26.6–13; Mark 14.3–9; Luke 7.36–50; John 12.1–9

> **Mark 14.1–9** It was two days before the Passover and the festival of Unleavened Bread. The chief priests and the scribes were looking for a way to arrest Jesus by stealth and kill him; ²for they said, 'Not during the festival, or there may be a riot among the people.' ³While he was at Bethany in the house of Simon the leper, as he sat at the table, a woman came with an alabaster jar of very costly ointment of nard, and she broke open the jar and poured the ointment on his head. ⁴But some were there who said to one another in anger, 'Why was the ointment wasted in this way? ⁵For this ointment could have been sold for more than three hundred denarii, and the money given to the poor.' And they scolded her. ⁶But Jesus said, 'Let her alone; why do you trouble her? She has performed a good service for me. ⁷For you always have the poor with you, and you can show kindness to them whenever you wish;

> but you will not always have me. [8]She has done what she could;
> she has anointed my body beforehand for its burial. [9]Truly I tell
> you, wherever the good news is proclaimed in the whole world,
> what she has done will be told in remembrance of her.'

Each of the Gospels has a story of the anointing of Jesus by a
woman and Christian tradition, over the years, has done such a
harmonizing job on these four accounts that it is hard, now, to
see clearly the themes that they bring. A small table may help in
clarifying the details:

	Matthew 26.6–13	Mark 14.3–9	Luke 7.36–50	John 12.1–9
Location	Bethany	Bethany	Galilee	Bethany
Host	Simon the leper	Simon the leper	Simon the Pharisee	Lazarus
Identity of the woman	A woman	A woman	A woman of the city	Mary
Body part anointed	Head	Head	Feet	Feet
Objection to the anointing came from	The disciples	Someone	Simon	Judas
Significance of the anointing	Burial	Burial	Knowledge of her need of forgiveness	Burial

As is now widely recognized, the conflation of these accounts led
into conflating Mary, sister of Lazarus, with Mary of Magdala
(possibly because she is mentioned in Luke 8.2, the passage
immediately following the Lukan account of anointing). This
conflation, first suggested by Ephraem in the fourth century, was
what gave rise to the tradition of Mary of Magdala being a pros-
titute (since it was assumed that the sin referred to by Luke was
prostitution). This conflation is rightly rejected today as being not
only unhelpful but untrue. However, the question remains what,
if any, connection exists between the accounts?

Anointing of head vs feet

The tradition of anointing the head with oil is well known in the Bible (Psalm 23.5 and Amos 6.6) as a sign of blessing to the recipient. It marks both celebration and relationship and would have been easily understood as such. Psalm 133.2 even suggests that you could pour quite a lavish amount of oil on the head as a part of this, though a whole bottle of oil takes even that lavishness to extremes.

What is harder to understand is the purpose of anointing feet. There is no evidence anywhere else that this was done. Washing feet, as we know from John 13, was common and expected but anointing feet was not. Commentators on Luke 7 attempt to explain the occurrence in terms of opportunity. As Jesus ate, he reclined with his feet behind him. As a result they were all the woman could reach as she entered the room and, being overwhelmed with emotion, began weeping and hence washing his feet with her tears. The anointing simply followed on the back of the tears. This may be the best explanation with the added element of reverence that washing feet implies.

It is worth noting that without John's account, Luke's account of anointing would be regarded as being so different from that of Matthew and Mark that they would not be considered together at all. It is John's account that acts as a middle term between the two, locating the event in Bethany as do Matthew and Mark and having Jesus' feet anointed as Luke does. It is impossible to work out whether these accounts are telling really quite different versions of the same event or similar versions of different events.

All we can do is to look at what function they have in the text at this point. We will look at the Matthew, Mark and John accounts as they are the ones that fit into the timescale that we are exploring. Matthew's and John's accounts focus our attention quite firmly on the prediction of Christ's death but Mark's Gospel adds an additional element as well. In Mark Jesus proclaims the woman's action as, in Greek, a *kalon ergon* which is translated in the NRSV as a good deed (though the word *kalon* has more of a sense of 'noble' about it).

An alabaster jar of pure nard

The receptacle for the nard is called an '*alabastros*' in Greek which simply means a perfume bottle, but since perfume bottles were often made from alabaster (hence their name) it is probable that it was made from alabaster.

The contents of the jar were spikenard oil. This is oil made from a plant that only grows in the foothills of the Himalayas (in China, Tibet and Nepal). As a result then, as now, the oil was vastly expensive.

Only Mark's Gospel has the detail that the woman smashed the jar before pouring it on Jesus' head. Some suggest that she did this as a means of getting the oil out, but it is more likely to be a sign that she intended from the start to use it all.

As a result Mark picks up a strand that has bubbled through much of the Gospel. In Mark when groups respond to Jesus they invariably react wrongly: the leaders are always opposed, the crowd mostly amazed and the disciples confused. In contrast individuals, who know their need of God, respond to Jesus as he is and recognize him to be who he is. This unnamed, unknown woman is a perfect example of such a reaction. It is unlikely that she intended to prepare Jesus for burial. Much more likely is that she wanted to respond to Jesus with an action of generosity that symbolized the depth of her response to who he was. As a result, this little cameo before the preparations for the last supper sheds light on the whole sweep of events that have happened up to this point. Time and time again the leaders have opposed Jesus, the crowd responded but then melted away, the disciples did their best, but demonstrated their continuing lack of understanding of Jesus. One woman alone illustrated with actions far more power-ful than words could have done that she understood who Jesus was and, understanding, that she wanted to respond to him with every fibre of her being.

* * *

Reflection

It is striking to notice at this point in the Gospel that of all the interactions that Jesus had in this last week of his life, the two that stand out involve two entirely unconnected women. The first, the widow with her gift, does not actually interact with Jesus himself but with God in the temple. Although she didn't need to, this widow came to the temple to display her love for God in giving far more than she could afford. In this way she is linked to the other unnamed woman who anointed Jesus with ridiculously expensive oil. Just like the widow, this other woman was driven to an act of insane generosity in response to her encounter with the insane generosity of God.

It is these two actions that bring into full focus the dynamic of the discomfort that an encounter with God and God's generosity evokes. As we read through this last week of Jesus' life, it becomes clear how much Jesus undermined the expectations of those who had waited for so long for the king-figure like David to arrive. The problem was that they knew what they wanted; they knew what they needed and, as is so often the case with God, what God offered was not what they expected.

It is easy for us to be dismissive of the Jewish authorities. Why could they not have seen Jesus for who he really was? Were they so blind that they couldn't accept the gift that he did bring rather than rejecting him entirely? The answer was no they couldn't and they couldn't because they had too much to lose. The authorities were attempting to achieve the finest of fine balancing acts between staying faithful to their Jewish heritage and beliefs while doing as little as they could to antagonize an oppressive empire that simply didn't understand who they were as a people. The pressures of the day, the political complexities involved and the pure fear that the Roman Empire evoked all meant that they simply could not afford to think differently. Jesus represented a completely different way of being, thinking and doing and what he represented risked unbalancing this finely honed existence. Rather than wondering why most of the Jewish authorities couldn't recognize him to be who he was, we should instead be amazed that some of them, such as Nicodemus or Joseph of Arimathea, could recognize him.

Jesus' own self was unsettling and discomforting and those who could truly respond to him were invariably, like the woman with the oil, people with the least to lose. All of this brings us to a vital reflection for Holy Week – what things prevent us from encountering Jesus as he really is rather than as we might want him to be? What is too important to us and so prevents us from meeting and responding to the real Jesus? The opinions of others? Prestige? Buildings? Anxiety?

The list could go on and on but now as then we need to be prepared to acknowledge that Jesus unsettles and discomforts us. The salvation that he brings requires us to change in ways we cannot foresee and probably don't want. A real encounter with Jesus should always leave us feeling profoundly uncomfortable. We should feel deep sympathy for the authorities of Jesus' day who were so caught up in what was going on that they simply could not recognize God when he appeared in their midst. Now as then, those who find it easiest to recognize Jesus for who he really is are those who have the least to lose.

On Hosannas

We cry Hosanna,
  and praise you for all your acts of goodness in days gone by
We cry Hosanna
  and plead for salvation still to come far off in the future

We cry Hosanna
  but we're not sure we meant now,
  and here is a little inconvenient,
  and we certainly didn't mean like this.

We cry Hosanna
  praying that the salvation when it comes will be comfortable,
    predictable and safe,
    that it won't tax us too far,
      won't be inconvenient in its demands

We cry Hosanna
  but it takes a woman silently bringing in her gift of ridiculous
    generosity,
  to pour down true Hosannas on Jesus

  Hosannas that, looking backwards in thanksgiving and
      forwards in hope
    embrace right now all that Jesus came to be ...
  Hosannas based not on what Jesus should be but on who he
    was and is.

As the Hosannas fade away beneath the shadow of the cross,
  Jesus hangs offering the salvation that so many cried for
  and then suddenly weren't sure if they wanted after all.

2

The Last Supper

The Plot against Jesus and Judas' Promise of Betrayal

Matthew 26.1–5, 14–16; Mark 14.1–2, 10–11; Luke 22.1–6

Mark 14.1-2 It was two days before the Passover and the festival of Unleavened Bread. The chief priests and the scribes were looking for a way to arrest Jesus by stealth and kill him; [2]for they said, 'Not during the festival, or there may be a riot among the people.'

Mark 14.10-11 Then Judas Iscariot, who was one of the twelve, went to the chief priests in order to betray him to them. [11]When they heard it, they were greatly pleased, and promised to give him money. So he began to look for an opportunity to betray him.

The introduction to the last supper in Matthew, Mark and Luke all focus our attention on the inevitability of Jesus' death. Mark and Luke keep that focus just on the chief priests and scribes (two out of the three groups that made up the Sanhedrin; for more on the Sanhedrin, see p. 76 below), but Matthew introduces, before this, an additional prophecy by Jesus about his death: 'When Jesus had finished saying all these things, he said to his disciples, "You know that after two days the Passover is coming, and the Son of Man will be handed over to be crucified"' (26.1–2). In Matthew, Jesus, as well as the chief priests and scribes, begins looking towards his death.

Not during the festival

The little phrase 'not during the festival' raises a much more important question about the timing of what went on here. The implication in both Matthew's and Mark's Gospels is that the chief priests were keen to capture Jesus but not during the feast itself (which we should probably take to be the whole eight-day festival). Their nervousness about this is understandable. There are differing accounts of how many people crowded into Jerusalem for the Passover. Rabbinic accounts suggest 12 million people; Josephus a more conservative 3 million; Jeremias proposes 180,000 people, but given that the normal population would have been around 30,000 even the most conservative figure represents a huge increase of population for these eight days.

Both the Jewish authorities and the Romans had much to gain in preventing any level of upset during Passover and this seems to lie behind their desire not to kill Jesus during the festival. The problem is that, if we go with accepted timings for Jesus' death, it did take place during the festival itself.

The timing of the last supper and hence of Jesus' death

The key question about timing is whether the last supper was a Passover meal or not. The washing of the disciples' feet in John 13, which is admittedly a very different account and shares with the Synoptic accounts only that the events take place at a meal shortly before Jesus' death, is explicitly not the Passover meal since in John's Gospel Jesus is killed on Nissan 14 not on Nissan 15. In other words, in John's Gospel Jesus died at the same time as the Passover lambs are being slaughtered in preparation for the Passover meal. So the meal there happened a whole day earlier than the meal in Matthew, Mark and Luke. The significance for this is that it is much easier to believe that the Sanhedrin met, had a trial and visited Pilate on the day *before* the full feast of Passover, than on the first day of this major festival (which would be the case if the last supper were the Passover meal).

It would also make much more sense of Matthew's and Mark's comments that the chief priests and scribes didn't want to do this during the festival (the answer being they didn't, they did it just before). Some scholars suggest as a result that, although not technically being a Passover meal, the last supper was a Passover meal in intention but eaten early because of Jesus' anxiety that he would not be able to eat the Passover meal with his followers. This might be implied in Luke 22:15: 'He said to them, "I have eagerly desired to eat this Passover with you before I suffer."' They also argue that this explains the apparent lack of a Passover lamb in the meal; they didn't have one because the lambs had not yet been slaughtered.

Was the last supper a Passover meal?

It is worth dropping in at this point that some scholars argue vehemently that the last supper is *not* a Passover meal. The reasons for this include the dating problems, but also the lack of a mention of a Passover lamb or bitter herbs which both form an essential part of that meal. Some argue that what is described is simply an unusual but ordinary Jewish meal at which the breaking of bread and sharing of a cup would have taken place because such things would have happened at those meals. They also argue that the later Christian community inscribed the last supper with Passover resonances because of the theological importance of understanding Jesus as instigating a new exodus.

For more on this see Jonathan Klawans's 'Was Jesus' Last Supper a Seder?' (*Bible Review*, October 2001). The article is also freely available on www.biblicalarchaeology.org/

The problem of course is that it is so important to our (and indeed the Synoptic writers) understanding of the last supper that it *was* the Passover meal, that suggesting it might not have been raises significant difficulties. We are left then with an unresolvable conundrum that we need to acknowledge before moving on.

- If we accept the traditional view that the last supper is the Passover meal then we have to suppose that the chief priests changed their minds and decided it was all right to kill Jesus during the feast after all and that their desire to do so over-rode other considerations about doing all this on the first, very solemn day of a major festival.
- If we accept a change of date to the day before the festival began, then the last supper, as in John's Gospel, is an antici-pation of the Passover meal not the actual Passover meal.

In my view the Passover resonances are so deeply important to the story that it is hard to remove them without fundamentally changing the narrative, but it is a view worth reflecting on. A very helpful discussion of all the options can be found in R. T. France's *New International Greek Testament Commentary* (Eerdmans, 2002, pp. 559–63).

The Feast of Passover and of Unleavened Bread

It is helpful to be clear about these two feasts, not least because the Gospel writers are not. Originally the feast of the Passover proper was around 12 hours long. On Nissan 14 the lambs were slaughtered in preparation for the Passover meal, which began after sunset that day (that is, Nissan 15, since days in Judaism begin in the evening). Later in the day of Nissan 15 the Feast of Unleavened Bread began and lasted for seven days. However, after the exile these two originally separate feasts were joined together which is why the Gospel writers refer to them as though they were the same thing. Mark's reference in verse 1 to the chief priests plotting to kill Jesus two days before the Passover and feast of Unleavened Bread suggests that this is referring to Nissan 13, but his subsequent reference in verse 12 to the preparations taking place on the first day of Unleavened Bread is confusing and probably should be taken to refer to Nissan 14.

A small point is that Luke 24, the story of the road to Emmaus, recounts Jesus breaking bread once they reached the house of

the disciples. As it would still have been the Feast of Unleavened Bread the question is what kind of bread did he break? Was
this the unleavened bread of the festival or older leavened bread
which due to the upheaval of Jesus' death had not been removed
from the house at the start of the feast?

Judas' decision to betray Jesus

One of the key questions surrounding Judas' decision and subsequent action is how culpable Judas should be seen to be. Some
scholars have argued that Judas' actions were not intended to
be hostile but that he intended to bring Jesus and the authorities
together in discussion, an action which went badly wrong. An
exploration of the Gospel texts indicates that this is probably not
a view held by any of the Gospel writers but that the level of his
culpability is read differently in the four Gospels.

Matthew and Mark both have Judas' decision to betray Jesus
immediately after the anointing of Jesus' feet by the unnamed
woman. In Mark's Gospel, Judas is at best a bit player in the narrative as a whole and his decision to betray Jesus came directly
after the anointing of Jesus by the woman, but Mark draws little
overt connection between the two. The two events are joined by
the word 'and' and so do not really imply causation. In Mark
Judas certainly betrays Jesus but Mark makes very little attempt
to explain why.

Matthew's Gospel likewise has Judas' decision following on
from the anointing, but connects the two with 'then' rather than
'and'. The word 'then' is a chronological word so it implies that
Judas' decision came after this event. This could imply that Jesus'
response to the woman contributed to Judas' decision, but the
word is not strong enough to make this clear. Matthew's Gospel,
however, is the one that states explicitly that Judas is paid with
thirty pieces of silver (a reference which suggests he was paid in
Tyrian silver coins or the temple tax money, see p. 29 above). This

hints that Judas' concern was financial and ties the decision, at least in part, to the anointing.

Luke's Gospel decouples Judas' decision from the anointing entirely. As a result he, like John's Gospel, provided an alternative explanation for Judas' actions: that Satan entered him (22.3). A similar explanation is offered by John (13.2) who nevertheless also is the one who makes the suggestion that Judas' disaffection was governed by money (12.4).

Iscariot

Although the Gospel writers themselves never make this connection, some scholars have wondered whether Judas' decision to betray Jesus can be attributed to his origins. The name Iscariot is often thought to come from the Hebrew for 'man of Kerioth'. If this is true then it is likely that Judas was the only disciple who came from Judah and not Galilee. Some scholars have wondered whether this contributed to his disaffection with Jesus.

The question of why Judas did what he did is not easily answered, and the Gospel writers, just like us, seem to have wrestled with the question of how much he was to blame. Mark doesn't answer the question at all; Matthew gives the merest hint that the motivation might be financial. Oddly the two Gospels that are clearest about why he did it – Luke and John – excuse his actions a little by attributing the action to Satan who entered him.

* * *

Reflection

Judas has always been a character that haunts me, and over the years I have discovered that I am not alone. The easy, superficial caricature of him is that he was bad through and through; he was a 'betrayer', always was and always would be. As we all know, however, these kinds of static judgements about people never capture the complete truth. Just as we are told not to say to our children that they are 'naughty', rather that they do naughty things, so we cannot write off Judas as a betrayer. What is interesting is that the Gospels don't either.

John's Gospel is the one that comes closest to suggesting that Judas was always a bad sort, hence attributing the criticism of the woman with the oil to him and him alone, but the others are less clear about it. Indeed I get the impression that the Gospel writers, and those to whom they talked, were as unclear about why Judas acted as he did as we are.

When we transfer the question to ourselves – why do we do those things that we don't intend to do but end up doing? – it becomes a lot easier to understand. Sometimes we have no idea at all why it is that we acted in the way that we did. Sometimes we can look back and trace a growing disaffection or anger which suddenly boils over and causes us to react; sometimes we allow ourselves to be taken over by external dynamics or forces. I wonder if Judas himself knew why he did it? Had he, as some suggest, acted out of good motives, hoping to reconcile Jesus and the authorities? Was he overcome by transitory irritation? Had he intended to betray Jesus for a long time and was simply waiting for his moment? As with many questions about this week, we simply cannot know the reasons why Judas did as he did, but he stands as a warning to each one of us that following Jesus in and of itself will not prevent us from acting with catastrophic consequences. None of us are that different from Judas. We all have the potential within us for betrayal and must keep forever on our lips the disciples' cry of horror 'surely not I, Lord' – let it not be me.

The Preparation of the Meal

Matthew 26.17–20; Mark 14.12–16; Luke 22.7–14

Mark 14.12–16 On the first day of Unleavened Bread, when the Passover lamb is sacrificed, his disciples said to him, 'Where do you want us to go and make the preparations for you to eat the Passover?' [13]So he sent two of his disciples, saying to them, 'Go into the city, and a man carrying a jar of water will meet you; follow him, [14]and wherever he enters, say to the owner of the house, 'The Teacher asks, "Where is my guest room where I may eat the Passover with my disciples?" [15]He will show you a large room upstairs, furnished and ready. Make preparations for us there.' [16]So the disciples set out and went to the city, and found everything as he had told them; and they prepared the Passover meal.

As with the finding of the donkey before the triumphal entry, Jesus appears to have made prior arrangements for the Passover meal. This was a sensible course of action given the number of people in Jerusalem for the festival, but again raises questions of how he did it, whose house it was and how Jesus knew them given that most of his ministry took place in Galilee (if we believe the Synoptic accounts). These are questions to which we cannot know the answer but it is clear that the plan is well thought out and that the man with the water jar was actively waiting for the disciples to show them where to go.

One of the important features of Jesus' instruction to the disciples is that the room allocated for them was 'furnished' and ready. This hints that the furniture was relatively formal dining furniture and hence that the house owner may have been wealthy. This is supported in Mark 14.18, where, although the NRSV says that Jesus and his disciples 'took their places', the Greek has that they 'reclined'.

Reclining to eat

While we cannot know for sure how Jews of the first century would have eaten, and formal meals in wealthy houses would have been very different from meals in rural Galilee, it is worth reminding ourselves that the word used in verse 18 (*anakeimai*; and indeed in a number of other places throughout the Gospels) for 'sitting at the table' actually means reclining. This implies that in wealthy houses at least the Graeco-Roman practice of lying down to eat was used.

Images from Graeco-Roman artwork indicate that the couches faced into a central table so that people's heads would have been together in the centre of the room and their feet behind them at the outer edges. This may explain in Luke 7 why the woman of the city anointed Jesus' feet – they were what she could reach easily when coming in from outside.

The next question that emerges is how many people were present? Christian tradition is clear that there are just thirteen people in the room: Jesus and his twelve male disciples. However, Mark goes out of his way to point out that Jesus had found for himself and his followers a 'large' room (in Greek *mega*). This may suggest that, in fact, there were many more people present than just thirteen. Indeed given the regular mention of the women who followed and supported Jesus throughout the Gospels, and the fact that a number of them were also present at the crucifixion, we do need to ask where they ate their Passover meal if not with Jesus and the other disciples.

Connected to this is the fact that Jesus sent two of his disciples to prepare the room (14.13) and then in verse 17 arrived with the twelve. Were those disciples part of the twelve or additional to them? Given the specific mention of the twelve in verse 17 it is most likely that the disciples mentioned in verse 13 were extra. What this does is to emphasize that the twelve were there with Jesus but that others may well have been present too. If this is the case it explains a small detail of the text which is that Judas was able to leave the group unnoticed, despite warnings that someone would betray Jesus. This is much more likely if the group were larger than just thirteen.

The *kataluma*

A brief point worthy of note is that in Mark's and Luke's Gospels the last supper took place in a guest room (*kataluma*). Anyone who is familiar with debates about the birth narratives in Luke will recall that Jesus was laid in a manger because there was no room for him in the *kataluma* (Luke 2.7). Popular Christian tradition has this as an inn but most New Testament scholars would argue that it is a guest room, or space in the house used for guests. This is certainly how it is being used in the account about preparations for the last supper.

In Bethlehem, depending on the size of the house, the *kataluma* may well have been little more than a corner of the upstairs living space, with the animals and their 'manger' below on the ground floor. In Jerusalem it is more likely that the *kataluma* was in fact a proper room.

One can't help wondering whether in Luke's mind at least there is a resonance with the birth narratives here. At Jesus' birth there was no room in the *kataluma*; just prior to his death he arranged his own *kataluma* for this most important farewell.

---

* * *

Reflection

We all know so well the stories surrounding Jesus' death, and as they are vividly and regularly depicted in art and film there will be few of us who do not have an inner gallery which shows us what those events looked like. Da Vinci, in particular, shapes our imaginings of what the last supper might have been like. It is hard to picture the last supper without having the disciples and Jesus all sitting up along one side of a table, facing in the same direction. Even though we know that it wouldn't look like that (Mark says explicitly that the disciples were reclining not sitting up) it is hard to remove its image from our inner gallery.

Part of the task of accompanying Jesus devotionally during the last week of his life is the task of repopulating our inner art galleries with new images of what it might have looked and felt like. It is worth taking the time deliberately and carefully to reimagine the last supper: with Jesus and his disciples lying rather than sitting and with a room possibly inhabited by more than thirteen people as initial details (though many more are possible too). Indeed it is this creative reimagining which can help us enter more fully into the events surrounding Jesus' death and accompany him more intentionally on his journey to the cross and beyond.

The Last Supper

Matthew 26.17–30; Mark 12.17–26; Luke 22.8–39

Writing about the last supper is something of a challenge. So much has been said and so much could be said that it is difficult to know where to begin. Even more than elsewhere in this book, then, I want to stress that the material covered here will be those themes that particularly interest me – there will be many gaps as it is impossible to cover everything that could be said.

Mark 14.17–26 When it was evening, he came with the twelve. [18]And when they had taken their places and were eating, Jesus said, 'Truly I tell you, one of you will betray me, one who is eating with me.' [19]They began to be distressed and to say to him one after another, 'Surely, not I?' [20]He said to them, 'It is one of the twelve, one who is dipping bread into the bowl with me. [21]For the Son of Man goes as it is written of him, but woe to that one by whom the Son of Man is betrayed! It would have been better for that one not to have been born.'

[22]While they were eating, he took a loaf of bread, and after blessing it he broke it, gave it to them, and said, 'Take; this is my body.' [23]Then he took a cup, and after giving thanks he gave it to them, and all of them drank from it. [24]He said to them, 'This is my blood of the covenant, which is poured out for many. [25]Truly I tell you, I will never again drink of the fruit of the vine until that day when I drink it new in the kingdom of God.' [26]When they had sung the hymn, they went out to the Mount of Olives.

The discussion about betrayal

Matthew and Mark both begin their accounts of the last supper with the discussion between Jesus and the disciples about who would betray Jesus. In contrast Luke includes this discussion with a range of other topics at the end of the meal before they went out to Gethsemane. Likewise John embeds the discussion in a much longer discourse which stretches over a number of chapters. Only in John is Judas explicitly identified as the 'betrayer', though even there the other disciples misunderstand what was going on.

Paradidōmi

The word translated as betray here is *paradidōmi*. As well as meaning 'betray' this word can also mean 'handed over' and as such is used throughout the Passion narrative to refer to what happened to Jesus. Jesus prophesies that he will be 'handed over' to death; he was handed over by Judas, by the religious authorities (Matthew 27.2, 18) and by Pilate (27.26). Judas' role in this whole process is highlighted only because what he did is translated as betrayed rather than handed over as elsewhere. Without wanting to exonerate Judas unnecessarily, the seriousness attributed to his action is heightened by the insistence of translating *paradidōmi* when it refers to him with the word 'betray' and when it refers to others with the phrase 'hand over'. It may be that our insistence on Judas' betrayal is influenced at least in part by our English translations.

It is important to notice that the verb *paradidōmi* emphasizes Jesus' passive role in all of this. Judas, the authorities and Pilate all handed Jesus over; in John's Gospel alone the verb is used actively to refer to Jesus' handing over of his spirit in 19.30 when he died. Only in John is Jesus portrayed as an active character in control of his own fate.

The words of institution

One of the important features to notice about the wording of the accounts about the last supper is that the words that are now used in services of Holy Communion are a mixture of Matthew, Mark, Luke and Paul.

- **Matthew 26.26–28** While they were eating, Jesus took a loaf of bread, and after blessing it he broke it, gave it to the disciples, and said, 'Take, eat; this is my body.' [27]Then he took a cup, and after giving thanks he gave it to them, saying, 'Drink from it, all of you; [28]for this is my blood of the covenant, which is poured out for many for the forgiveness of sins.'
- **Mark 14.22–24** While they were eating, he took a loaf of bread, and after blessing it he broke it, gave it to them, and said, 'Take; this is my body.' [23]Then he took a cup, and after giving thanks he gave it to them, and all of them drank from it. [24]He said to them, 'This is my blood of the covenant, which is poured out for many.'
- **Luke 22.17–20** Then he took a cup, and after giving thanks he said, 'Take this and divide it among yourselves; [18]for I tell you that from now on I will not drink of the fruit of the vine until the kingdom of God comes.' [19]Then he took a loaf of bread, and when he had given thanks, he broke it and gave it to them, saying, 'This is my body, which is given for you. Do this in remembrance of me.' [20]And he did the same with the cup after supper, saying, 'This cup that is poured out for you is the new covenant in my blood.'
- **1 Corinthians 11.23–25** For I received from the Lord what I also handed on to you, that the Lord Jesus on the night when he was betrayed took a loaf of bread, [24]and when he had given thanks, he broke it and said, 'This is my body that is for you. Do this in remembrance of me.' [25]In the same way he took the cup also, after supper, saying, 'This cup is the new covenant in my blood. Do this, as often as you drink it, in remembrance of me.'

Only 1 Corinthians has the double command to 'do this in remembrance of me'. Luke does contain this command but only in relation to the bread and not the cup. All the accounts tie the cup to a new covenant, but only Matthew associates the blood with forgiveness of sins. One of the key questions – to which, surprisingly enough there is no easy answer – is why Mark has no explicit command that the disciples are to eat or drink and why neither Matthew nor Mark have a command that this action should be continued as a memorial of Jesus' death.

The argument from silence is a difficult one to make. Many liturgists would argue that Mark and Matthew were written so long after 1 Corinthians that they omitted the remembrance command because they knew that everyone already knew it. This may well be the case, and Mark's words 'Take, this is my body' are so truncated that it is not impossible to propose that they implied much more than is actually included, but it is impossible to state this with certainty. It is also possible that he omitted them because he wasn't aware of that tradition.

Breaking and blessing bread

Jesus breaks bread and gives thanks on many occasions throughout the Gospels, so much so, in fact, that some people assume it was his trademark action. So, for example, when he broke the bread in the story of the road to Emmaus, it is often assumed that it was simply that action that identified him to the confused disciples. The problem with this is that breaking and blessing bread at the start of a meal was the normal, expected action of the father of the family or the host at the meal. Jewish meals simply began with breaking and blessing bread. The only way it would have identified Jesus specifically was if he had an unusual way of doing it.

Much more important is that Jesus' action of breaking and blessing bread symbolized his role as father of the community and host at the meal.

The effect of the lack of the remembrance command, however, is to focus the whole story much more onto Jesus' death than on the command to remember him. His blood poured out for many (which Matthew glosses as meaning 'the forgiveness of sins') in Mark's and Matthew's accounts become the central focus of the whole story. When we place this alongside the words that would normally be said over the cups at a Jewish Passover meal, the

JOURNEY TO THE EMPTY TOMB

significance of what is happening here is brought into sharp relief. The blood of the Passover lamb was daubed on the doors of the people of God so that the angel of the Lord would 'pass-over' their houses and not kill the first born. Here the blood of the new covenant evokes a new 'passing-over', a passing over that Matthew associates particularly with sin. This focuses our attention more on the event of salvation than on the act of remembering it.

Remembrance

In contrast Paul, even more than Luke, focuses our attention on the act of remembrance. The double command to 'do this in remembrance of me' places the focus much more on the continued memorial than on the original event. This is hardly surprising in 1 Corinthians 11 since there Paul is talking about *how* the Corinthian community remember the event and reminding them of the importance of doing this well and with good order.

Remembrance is an important word here. It is well known that the Greek word *anamnesis*, especially when used in liturgical settings, is thought to have a greater significance than just 'calling to mind'. The act of *anamnesis* is to make the event present again by your actions. So Jesus' command to do this in *anamnesis* of him is so powerfully to recall the event of the last supper by our words and actions that we make it present in our midst.

This is what the original Passover meal also did. The words and actions used at the Passover meal served to make the first Passover present. The events of fleeing from Egypt were brought so vividly to mind in the present that it was as though it were happening again. It wasn't just about looking backwards. Those celebrating the Passover also looked forward to a future moment when God would once more intervene in the world (hence the wish 'next year in Jerusalem' that is said at the end of each Passover meal today). 'Remembering' then involves collapsing time in on itself so that past event and future salvation meet in the present.

Exactly the same thing happens in the last supper. Every time we do this 'in remembrance of him' we bring Jesus' death and future return together in the present, looking backwards in a thanksgiving and forwards in a hope that transforms our lives in the present.

The conundrum of the cups

> **Luke 22.17–20** Then he took a cup, and after giving thanks he said, 'Take this and divide it among yourselves; [18]for I tell you that from now on I will not drink of the fruit of the vine until the kingdom of God comes.' [19]Then he took a loaf of bread, and when he had given thanks, he broke it and gave it to them, saying, 'This is my body, which is given for you. Do this in remembrance of me.' [20]And he did the same with the cup after supper, saying, 'This cup that is poured out for you is the new covenant in my blood.'

In some ways, Luke's account acts as a mid-point between Matthew and Mark, and Paul's account of the institution of the last supper. Luke also focuses our attention on the last supper as a new Passover meal but in a slightly different way. He, like Paul, does have the command to remember but here it accompanies only the sharing of the bread, not the bread and the wine. Much more important in Luke is that Luke has two cups.

We are so accustomed to the structure of the last supper, as gleaned from Matthew, Mark and Paul, that it can be easy to overlook the profound difference of Luke's account. Whereas the others all have the breaking of the bread followed by the sharing of the cup, in Luke the sharing of the bread is both preceded *and* succeeded by a cup. The most likely explanation for this is that Luke is attempting to stay much closer to an overt connection with the Passover meal than is suggested by just one cup.

The challenge is to try and work out what the two cups signify. The problem is that it is almost impossible to know which of the traditions later associated with the Passover were in place in the first-century celebration of the Passover meal. Later tradition identifies four cups drunk at the Passover meal and some commentators associate these four cups with four theological themes drawn from Exodus 6.6–7.

> **Exodus 6.6–7** Say therefore to the Israelites, 'I am the Lord, and I will free you from the burdens of the Egyptians and deliver you from slavery to them. I will redeem you with an outstretched arm and with mighty acts of judgment. [7]I will take you as my people, and I will be your God. You shall know that I am the Lord your God, who has freed you from the burdens of the Egyptians.'

- First cup – the cup of sanctification (I will make you holy).
- Second cup – the cup of deliverance (I will free you).
- Third cup – the cup of redemption (I will redeem you).
- Fourth cup – the cup of hope (I will take you as my people).

This association, however, comes from traditions in the Jerusalem Talmud (on the dating of the Talmuds see below) and it is unclear whether this association was made as early as the first century. An earlier tradition found in the Mishnah Pesahim 10.1–7 also identifies four cups but does not tie them to Exodus 6.6–7. The Mishnah describes when in the meal the four cups are drunk and what is said around their preparation and it is noteworthy that the Mishnah is explicit that everyone, even the poor, should drink four cups of wine.

The Mishnah and the Talmuds

The Mishnah is a collection of sayings by Rabbis which is thought to have been written down around AD 200. Having said that, the sayings it contains are attributed to Rabbis who lived much earlier than this. It is therefore possible (though hard to prove) that at least some of the sayings it contains could come from the time of Jesus.

There are two Talmuds, the Jerusalem (or Palestinian) Talmud and the Babylonian Talmud. Both Talmuds contain additional reflections by Rabbis based on the earlier Mishnaic sayings. They are a kind of commentary on the Mishnah. The Jerusalem Talmud dates to around AD 400 and the Babylonian Talmud to around 100 years later. It is often very hard to know how far the traditions they contain stretch back. Some may date from as early as the New Testament but most are probably from a later period.

It is difficult, therefore, to assume that practices described in either of the Talmuds can give us insights into what happened at the time of Jesus.

Mishnah Pesahim describes the unfolding of the Passover feast thus: The feast began with the pouring of the first cup of wine. Over this cup the host blessed God for the wine and the day. This was followed by 'starters' described by the Mishnah as seasoned lettuce. Then the tables were brought forward and the food served but not eaten. This was when the second cup of wine was drunk and the first Hallel psalm (113) was sung. The main meal, including the lamb, was then eaten, along with the unleavened bread (which the host blessed) and bitter herbs. During the meal the question about the exodus ('what makes this night different from others nights?') was asked and answered. Following this, grace was said over the third cup of wine and the rest of the Hallel psalms (114–118) were sung in a context of praise that surrounded also the fourth cup of wine.

Hallelujah

As many people will know, the Hallel psalms and the word 'Hallelujah' are closely connected. Although not only used in the Hallel psalms, Hallelujah literally means 'praise the Lord' ('hallelu' is the plural command to praise and 'jah' a shortening of the name of God).

Jesus' last meal then was, somewhat poignantly, set against a background of praise.

Some people may be aware of a fifth cup, poured but not drunk and left for Elijah. This, like the association with Exodus 6.6–7, seems to be a much later tradition. There is no evidence at all that this was practised at the time of Jesus.

One strong connection between the Mishnah's account of the Passover meal and Jesus' last supper is the mention in Matthew and Mark of the singing of a 'hymn' which may well refer to the Hallel psalms (Psalms 113–118) which were to be started during the meal and finished at the end. It is fascinating to note that one of these would have been Psalm 118 – the psalm sung during Jesus' entry into Jerusalem.

The question, then, is which of the two cups mentioned in Luke match which of the four cups from the Mishnah? This is not as easy to answer as you might think. Luke's first cup is probably the first or the second Passover cup; and the second, the third or fourth. The reason for this is that the second cup is taken *after* the meal and so must be one of the post-meal cups. Some have suggested that they are the second and third cups, which they identify as the Talmud does as the cup of deliverance and the cup of redemption; attractive as this might be, there is no evidence that these cups were associated like this at the time of Jesus.

It is hardly surprising that Luke's two cups have not passed into common Christian usage but it is nevertheless important to take some time to reflect on their presence and significance in his narrative.

Drinking in the kingdom of God

Luke's two cups are not the only things omitted from common Christian use of the words of the last supper. The other words missing from the institution are the words that Jesus used when he looked forward to partaking of the fruit of the vine in the kingdom of God. These occur in the Gospels like this:

- **Matthew 26.29** 'I tell you, I will never again drink of this fruit of the vine until that day when I drink it new with you in my Father's kingdom.'
- **Mark 14.25** 'Truly I tell you, I will never again drink of the fruit of the vine until that day when I drink it new in the kingdom of God.'

- **Luke 22.18** 'For I tell you that from now on I will not drink of the fruit of the vine until the kingdom of God comes.'

But these words are missing from 1 Corinthians 11. In Luke's Gospel the words are slightly confusing as Jesus says them over the first cup he shared, which suggests that he did not partake in the second cup shared with his followers in verse 20. With these words, we are reminded that the ultimate horizon of existence is not what is about to happen to Jesus at his crucifixion but is instead the end of all times when there will be feasting without end. Many people take these words to be a looking forward to the Messianic banquet that will happen at the end of all time.

Beliefs about the Messianic banquet

The words 'Messianic banquet' refer to an understanding of

Isaiah 25.6–9 On this mountain the Lord of hosts will make for all peoples a feast of rich food, a feast of well-aged wines, of rich food filled with marrow, of well-aged wines strained clear. [7]And he will destroy on this mountain the shroud that is cast over all peoples, the sheet that is spread over all nations; [8]he will swallow up death forever. Then the Lord God will wipe away the tears from all faces, and the disgrace of his people he will take away from all the earth, for the Lord has spoken. [9]It will be said on that day, Lo, this is our God; we have waited for him, so that he might save us. This is the Lord for whom we have waited; let us be glad and rejoice in his salvation.

In this passage Isaiah looks forward to the future when God would return to his people and comfort them, and, Isaiah prophesies, there will be a sumptuous feast of food and wine. There are many times in Jesus' life when it looks as though the Messianic banquet has already begun but none more so than at the last supper, with its linking of the current meal with a time in the future when Jesus would feast in God's kingdom.

The words that look forward to Jesus' drinking wine in God's kingdom, like his other words, provide a new interpretation for this new form of Passover meal. The original Passover meal explained the significance of the event being commemorated and the food eaten. In the same way Jesus re-explained and reinterpreted the significance of the bread and wine in this new Passover commemoration. His words of interpretation are as important as the actions, since they provide the framework within which we are to remember what is going on.

The last supper reminds us that God is once more leading his people out of slavery and into freedom, a freedom that is achieved this time, not by the death of the firstborn sons of others, but by the death of his own, most beloved son. It also reminds us that in this freedom we look forward to the time in the age to come when we will feast with God in his kingdom. Every time we commemorate the last supper we look backwards to Jesus' death and forwards to the Messianic banquet and that action of remembering, of making present what is past and what is to come, transforms the present.

The washing of the disciples' feet in John's Gospel (John 13.1ff)

We cannot leave the events of the night before Jesus died without a brief foray into John's Gospel and all the complexities it presents.

We noted above that John's Gospel suggests a different timing for Jesus' last meal with his friends. One explanation for the different timing (and different actions) of the supper in the fourth Gospel is that it is, in fact, a different meal. The problem here is that there are sufficient markers to suggest that it is, in fact, the same event. The most important is the discussion about who would betray Jesus which is present in all four Gospels. Another significant overlap is the indication of a new covenant which is stated with the cup in the Synoptic Gospels and hinted at with the new commandment in John.

All in all it seems likely that these are meant to be the same event, which then raises the question of why John does not include the institution of the last supper here? A common and widely accepted answer is because that meal is so deeply woven into the fabric of the whole Gospel that it would be odd to 'institute' it here. In some ways John's Gospel can be read as a Gospel of the Eucharist with the twin themes of bread and wine woven around everything that Jesus said and did in his ministry.

This focuses our attention on the symbolic action that *is* included in John's Gospel: the washing of the disciples' feet. It is intriguing that one symbolic action – the meal together – has become a regularly practised action in Christian communities; whereas the other symbolic action – the washing of each other's feet – is often preserved for a service on Maundy Thursday (or for the ordination of deacons in some traditions). The irony here is that the first symbolic action – the Passover meal – was a once a year event and the second symbolic action – the washing of feet – a daily event. In Christian practice this has been switched: the Passover meal is now a weekly (sometimes daily) event and the washing of feet often just once yearly.

The washing of the disciples' feet is widely accepted to communicate self-sacrificial humility and as such, therefore, to be a prophetic action pointing to Jesus' ultimate sacrifice on the cross. When you recognize this, in my view, something important becomes clear. In John's Gospel the Eucharist is woven throughout the Gospel and Jesus' self-sacrificial humility indicated in the symbolic action at the last supper. In the Synoptic Gospels Jesus' self-sacrificial humility which will end in his death on the cross is woven throughout the Gospels and the Eucharist is indicated in the symbolic action at the last supper. The Gospels have the same themes, they have just woven them together in different ways.

Nevertheless, the effect of being communities that make our regular symbolic action the Eucharist is that the command to imitate Jesus in his self-sacrificial humility has become secondary. John's Gospel issues a ringing challenge to us all to reflect on what kind of communities we might be if we made an action of self-sacrificial humility of equal value to the action of remembrance when we structure our life together.

* * *

Reflection

There are occasions in the celebration of Christian faith when time collapses in on itself and we are invited to step outside humanity's linear timeframe and to enter God's eternal time. Our commemoration of Jesus' last supper with his disciples is definitely one of those times.

In it we are invited to look far back into history and to bring into the present the first exodus from slavery into freedom; we also look backwards to the moment of the second exodus when God's own son willingly died so he might lead God's people into freedom from sin. As we look back we bring into the present, we remember, reconstitute and proclaim God's historic actions in the world. At the same time we look forwards to the far horizon of time when we will join Jesus at the Messianic banquet and both he and we will, once more, be drinking of the fruit of the vine.

This looking backwards and forwards is more than just a memory and an anticipation, it is a making real in the present of events far distant, both past and future. As we remember, we transform the present, reminding ourselves not only that the God who brought his people from slavery into freedom will do so again and again but also that our feasting with Jesus is a joining-in now with the Messianic banquet. Celebrating the last supper holds together the past and the future in the present and in doing so it transforms us, God's people of freedom, to be people fit for his kingdom.

The remembering that we do in our commemoration of the last supper is the most momentous theological action that we are called to do as Christians. It is an action laden with meaning and significance, though fortunately we do not have to comprehend it in all its complexity in order to do it.

On Remembering

We remember and as we remember
    we place ourselves in the great chain of history,
    receiving, accepting and cherishing the history of God's own
        people
    and becoming a people called to a life of freedom

We remember and as we remember
    we place ourselves in the great chain of history
    looking forwards to the glorious feasting of the Messianic
        banquet
    and becoming a people shaped by the celebration of God's
        kingdom

We remember and as we remember
    we place ourselves in the great chain of history
    savouring the present in which past and future combine
    and becoming a people whose song is forever Hallelujah.

We remember and as we remember
    we shatter the chain of history and step into God's eternity
    In which there is no past, no present or future
    No beginning and no end
    only God and never-ending praise.

3

Gethsemane and the Trials

The Conversation after the Meal

Matthew 26.31–35; Mark 14.27–31; Luke 22.21–38

> **Mark 14.27-31** And Jesus said to them, 'You will all become deserters; for it is written, "I will strike the shepherd, and the sheep will be scattered." [28]But after I am raised up, I will go before you to Galilee.' [29]Peter said to him, 'Even though all become deserters, I will not.' [30]Jesus said to him, 'Truly I tell you, this day, this very night, before the cock crows twice, you will deny me three times.' [31]But he said vehemently, 'Even though I must die with you, I will not deny you.' And all of them said the same.

In both Matthew's and Mark's Gospels the last supper is followed by a conversation between Jesus and his disciples about Peter's denial of Jesus. In Luke and John this conversation takes place as part of the meal; whereas in Matthew and Mark it occurs after the meal and on the way to Gethsemane. The effect of Matthew's and Mark's placing of the story is that the last supper is bookended with prophesies of betrayal: it begins with the prophecy of Judas' betrayal and ends with the prophecy that all the disciples will let Jesus down. In short the concern of the disciples at the start of the last supper that they might be the one who betrays Jesus is confirmed here. They may not actually hand him over but they will nevertheless stumble in their discipleship.

Stumbling

The NRSV translates the verb in Mark 14.27 as 'desert' ('you will become deserters') but this does not quite do justice to the verb used here. The verb is the passive of *skandalizō* and so means something like 'to be led into stumbling' (hence the NIV chooses 'fall away'). The point is that they will all be caused to stumble in their discipleship but that beyond the stumbling there is hope and resurrection life.

In contrast, Luke's Gospel draws the discourse about betrayal and stumbling into a single conversation about the nature of discipleship generally (22.21–38). It starts at the meal and begins with Jesus' prophecy of betrayal, is followed by the dispute between the disciples about who is greatest, moves on to the prophecy about Peter's desertion (here he is identified as Simon) and ends with the command to ensure that they have swords. It is an extremely odd passage and scholars struggle to understand it. The key question is whether Jesus' 'It is enough' in 22.38 is a reprimand or a support of the disciples' statement that they have two swords.

Luke 22.21–38 'But see, the one who betrays me is with me, and his hand is on the table. ²²For the Son of Man is going as it has been determined, but woe to that one by whom he is betrayed!' ²³Then they began to ask one another which one of them it could be who would do this. ²⁴A dispute also arose among them as to which one of them was to be regarded as the greatest. ²⁵But he said to them, 'The kings of the Gentiles lord it over them; and those in authority over them are called benefactors. ²⁶But not so with you; rather the greatest among you must become like the youngest, and the leader like one who serves. ²⁷For who is greater, the one who is at the table or the one who serves? Is it not the one at the table? But I am among you as one who serves.

²⁸'You are those who have stood by me in my trials; ²⁹and I confer on you, just as my Father has conferred on me, a kingdom,

---

[30]so that you may eat and drink at my table in my kingdom, and you will sit on thrones judging the twelve tribes of Israel.

[31]'Simon, Simon, listen! Satan has demanded to sift all of you like wheat, [32]but I have prayed for you that your own faith may not fail; and you, when once you have turned back, strengthen your brothers.' [33]And he said to him, 'Lord, I am ready to go with you to prison and to death!' [34]Jesus said, 'I tell you, Peter, the cock will not crow this day, until you have denied three times that you know me.'

[35]He said to them, 'When I sent you out without a purse, bag, or sandals, did you lack anything?' They said, 'No, not a thing.' [36]He said to them, 'But now, the one who has a purse must take it, and likewise a bag. And the one who has no sword must sell his cloak and buy one. [37]For I tell you, this scripture must be fulfilled in me, "And he was counted among the lawless"; and indeed what is written about me is being fulfilled.' [38]They said, 'Lord, look, here are two swords.' He replied, 'It is enough.'

To my mind the best explanation is that the whole stretch of the conversation points to the increasing urgency of what is going on at this point. Even the disciples are falling into disarray: one of them will betray Jesus, the others fight over who is most important and Jesus states that all of them will desert him. The looming conflict is so great that they will find the need to protect themselves with a sword if necessary because Jesus will be seen as an evil-doer. As they so often do the disciples misunderstand Jesus and rummage around between them and discover that they have two swords between them all. Jesus' 'it is enough', then, is a reprimand, or more likely the equivalent of 'give me strength!' Even now at this point of Jesus' life (and forthcoming death) the disciples simply do not understand the importance or urgency of what is taking place. What they should be doing is preparing themselves for the cost of discipleship but instead they are squabbling about who is most important and missing the point of what Jesus is trying to tell them.

* * *

Reflection

One of the striking things about the way in which this part of the story is told is the fact that although only one disciple handed Jesus over, the other eleven did betray him in one way or another. The more vehement they were – Peter in particular – that they would not betray Jesus, the more they walked unseeing straight towards the event that would trip them all up and make them stumble. Matthew and Mark tell the story in a shorter way than Luke, but the same message comes through all three Gospels. The disciples simply didn't understand what faced Jesus – how could they? – but the more they thought they did understand, the more likely it was that they would be caused to stumble.

Luke's account, confusing though it may be, brings to the fore the ridiculousness of the disciples' obsessions: that evening they faced a tsunami of an event that would change their lives forever. Jesus' attempts to warn them of what was coming were faced with bravado ('of course *I* won't do that') and squabbling about who was the most important. It would be nice to say that we no longer do this – nice but entirely inaccurate. Even today we veer between self-justification and obsession with our own importance, when if only we could look up we would see the inevitable waves rushing towards us.

The point to hold onto is that the disciples did all stumble and the risen Jesus did go before them to Galilee. Fortunately discipleship is not negated by our own ridiculousness, our own failing and inabilities. We, like the disciples, will be caused to stumble, often by ourselves and our inability to recognize what is coming towards us, but beyond the stumbling there is the risen Christ who patiently waits for us to get to our feet once more, dust ourselves down and resume the self-sacrificial humble path of discipleship.

Jesus' Prayer in Gethsemane

Matthew 26.36–46; Mark 14.32–42; Luke 22.39–46

> **Mark 14.32-42** They went to a place called Gethsemane; and he said to his disciples, 'Sit here while I pray.' [33]He took with him Peter and James and John, and began to be distressed and agitated. [34]And he said to them, 'I am deeply grieved, even to death; remain here, and keep awake.' [35]And going a little farther, he threw himself on the ground and prayed that, if it were possible, the hour might pass from him. [36]He said, 'Abba, Father, for you all things are possible; remove this cup from me; yet, not what I want, but what you want.' [37]He came and found them sleeping; and he said to Peter, 'Simon, are you asleep? Could you not keep awake one hour? [38]Keep awake and pray that you may not come into the time of trial; the spirit indeed is willing, but the flesh is weak.' [39]And again he went away and prayed, saying the same words. [40]And once more he came and found them sleeping, for their eyes were very heavy; and they did not know what to say to him. [41]He came a third time and said to them, 'Are you still sleeping and taking your rest? Enough! The hour has come; the Son of Man is betrayed into the hands of sinners. [42]Get up, let us be going. See, my betrayer is at hand.'

The normal lodging place for Jesus and his disciples was Bethany (see Matthew 21.17; 26.6 for example) but according to Matthew and Mark Jesus did not return to Bethany on this night but went instead to Gethsemane. Although no one is absolutely clear about where Gethsemane was, there has been no dispute about its traditional location on the western slope just across the Kidron valley from Jerusalem. The significance of this position is that, while it was outside the city walls, unlike Bethany it still fell within the extended boundary of Jerusalem which was set during times of overcrowding such as the Passover. As a result, Jesus withdrew to a quiet place but did not leave Jerusalem.

Gethsemane

As mentioned above, no one is quite sure where Gethsemane was, but there may have been symbolic significance in its name. Many believe Gethsemane to come from the Aramaic *Gat-Smane* which means olive press. Thus it would have been the place where the olives from the Mount of Olives were brought to be pressed. As this was Jesus' great time of.'pressing' a connection might be made here.

Gethsemane is popularly called the garden of Gethsemane. It is worth noting that we get Gethsemane from Matthew and Mark and the garden from John. 'After Jesus had spoken these words, he went out with his disciples across the Kidron valley to a place where there was a garden' (John 18.1).

The whole story of Gethsemane is a story of human vulnerability. Centre stage is Jesus' own vulnerability. In both Matthew's and Mark's accounts he became grieved and distressed before he began to pray; in Luke his distress grew while he prayed until his sweat fell to the ground like drops of blood. In each of the Synoptic accounts there can be no doubt of the cost to Jesus in what he was about to do. The disciples are a foil to this. They also display human vulnerability but in a very different way. Despite their intentions, they fell asleep, unable to support Jesus in his time of agony. Matthew and Mark agree in emphasizing the extent of the disciples' human vulnerability by having them fall asleep three times while Jesus kept his lonely vigil; whereas in Luke this happens only once.

Jesus' agony in Gethsemane is the vital corrective against any assumption that he somehow willed his own death. There is no way that you can read of Jesus' vigil without being clear that Jesus did not wish to die, or to suffer what was about to come.

Jesus' agony in Luke's Gospel

Although there are a number of overlaps between Luke's account of Gethsemane and that of Matthew and Mark, there are also a number of important key differences. In Matthew and Mark, the story is focused, as mentioned above, around Jesus' distress. In Luke it is more focused around temptation. If you compare Jesus' words in Matthew and Mark with those in Luke the shift of focus is clear.

- **Mark 14.34**   And he said to them, 'I am deeply grieved, even to death; remain here, and keep awake.'
- **Matthew 26.36**   Then Jesus went with them to a place called Gethsemane; and he said to his disciples, 'Sit here while I go over there and pray.'
- **Luke 22.40**   When he reached the place, he said to them, 'Pray that you may not come into the time of trial.'

Jesus' distress is most evident in Mark; Luke is where the greatest stress is on temptation. This is an important strand in Luke. In Luke's temptation narratives, unlike in Matthew or Mark, Luke says that the devil departed from Jesus until the right time (*kairos* in Greek). As a result, the whole of Jesus' ministry is set in the context of temptation. This becomes even more important when you appreciate the nature of the temptations. The temptations were about what kind of ministry Jesus would have. Two out of the three temptations were prefaced by the phrase, 'If you are the Son of God … then …' Jesus' response indicated he was not that kind of Son of God: not one who would do miracles for his own benefit but for others, not one who would worship someone who was not God for personal gain, and not one who would test God.

Peirasmos

It is quite hard to see the theme of temptation running through Luke's Gospel in the NRSV because the word *peirasmos* is variously translated into English as test or trial. Some of the key places where it occurs are in the Parable of the Sower where the seed that falls on the rock is described as falling away 'in a time of testing' (Luke 8.13) and of course here where the disciples are told to pray that they do not face the same trial that Jesus does (22.40). It also gives more depth to plea in the Lord's Prayer that we are not brought to a time of trial (11.4). Jesus' trials throughout the Gospel show us how difficult it is to be brought to a time of trial and why it is that we should pray with such fervour that we are not brought to such times.

Placing Jesus' ministry in the context of temptation means that the whole of his ministry became a question of what kind of Son of God he would be, and continued, as we will see, up to his death on the cross. In Luke Jesus explicitly made this definition of his ministry in his post-meal conversation with the disciples when he said: 'You are those who have stood by me in my trials' (Luke 22.28). Jesus' twofold command to the disciples (22.40 and 46) reminds us one more time that Jesus continues to face temptations as he has from the outset of his ministry.

Sleeping because of grief

Luke is the only Gospel that offers the disciples overt mitigation for their inappropriate slumber. While in Matthew and Mark we are left to make up our own minds about why they were unable to stay awake, in Luke we are told that they fell asleep overwhelmed by grief. In other words we are to forgive them their desertion of Jesus this early on in his trial because of their grief.

Another feature peculiar to Luke's Gospel is the appearance of an angel in response to Jesus' prayer:

> **Luke 22.42–45** 'Father, if you are willing, remove this cup from me; yet, not my will but yours be done.' [43]Then an angel from heaven appeared to him and gave him strength. [44]In his anguish he prayed more earnestly, and his sweat became like great drops of blood falling down on the ground. [45]When he got up from prayer, he came to the disciples and found them sleeping because of grief.

The intriguing question is what 'strength' did the angel give to Jesus? His agony appeared to worsen rather than to lighten after the angelic appearance. This suggests that the strength the angel lent was the ability to look even deeper into the agony that faced him, rather than to feel better about it.

Jesus' prayer

Jesus' prayer is similar in all three Gospels.

- **Matthew 26.39**   'My Father, if it is possible, let this cup pass from me; yet not what I want but what you want.'
- **Mark 14.36**   He said, 'Abba, Father, for you all things are possible; remove this cup from me; yet, not what I want, but what you want.'
- **Luke 22.42**   'Father, if you are willing, remove this cup from me; yet, not my will but yours be done.'

The reference to God as Father is, of course, a supremely important point to note. It is the way in which Jesus spoke to God throughout his life and ministry and as such is unique. Although God is described as like a father in the Old Testament, and some Jews are described as sons of God, the direct and intimate address to God as father is not known before Jesus. This is why the Lord's Prayer (and Paul's similar reference in Romans 8.15 and Galatians 4.6) is so important. We are invited to address God as only Jesus has done before us, and in doing so to step into an intimate relationship with God never before articulated.

It is important not to overstate the intimacy, however. Abba is not the equivalent of 'daddy' as James Barr so famously argued in his 1988 article 'Abba is not daddy' (*JTS*, 38, 1988, 28–47). We should not impose modern Western informality onto Ancient Eastern relationships. Abba expresses formal intimacy, of son or daughter to father, but nothing more than that. Ancient Eastern relationships may have been close but were never informal.

Jesus' request that God remove the cup or let it pass from him is of course metaphorical but immediately brings to mind the cup of the last supper – the cup of Jesus' blood. What is important here is the recognition that Jesus, unlike some of the early Christian martyrs, did not relish what he was about to do. He was not rushing headlong into this but was obedient to his father and his father's will.

Jesus in the garden in John's Gospel

Given the moving nature of Jesus' distress that we encounter in Matthew, Mark and Luke, its lack in John's Gospel is even more obvious. There is no equivalent of the prayer in the garden in John 18. Barely have Jesus and his disciples entered the garden when Judas arrives, betrays Jesus and he is arrested. The closest episode to this is found much earlier in John 12.27–28, in the discussion between Jesus and some unnamed Greeks.

John 12.27–33 'Now my soul is troubled. And what should I say – "Father, save me from this hour"? No, it is for this reason that I have come to this hour. [28]Father, glorify your name.' Then a voice came from heaven, 'I have glorified it, and I will glorify it again.' [29]The crowd standing there heard it and said that it was thunder. Others said, 'An angel has spoken to him.' [30]Jesus answered, 'This voice has come for your sake, not for mine. [31]Now is the judgment of this world; now the ruler of this world will be driven out. [32]And I, when I am lifted up from the earth, will draw all people to myself.' [33]He said this to indicate the kind of death he was to die.

Jesus is hardly in agony there in the way he was in Gethsemane, but his expression of being troubled (the Greek word is *tarassō* which means to be stirred up, thrown into confusion or tossed about) indicates a much lesser degree of certainty than the Jesus of John's Gospel normally does. It is noticeable, however, that as soon as this uncertainty was expressed, God responded with reassurance. This is a very different picture to the Jesus who was strengthened by the angel to look more deeply into what was about to happen to him.

* * *

Reflection

The image of Jesus' agony in the garden is one that is profoundly affecting. John's Jesus who was supremely in control of events, knew exactly what he was doing and who suffered apparently only temporary anxiety (an anxiety immediately allayed by God), is far less moving than a Jesus who was wracked with grief and distress at the prospect of what he had to do. This distress seems to be heightened in Luke's Gospel by the angel who strengthened Jesus only for him to feel even more agony at the prospect of what was to come.

This suggests that there is more to comfort than simply making people feel better. Indeed the Latin word *conforto,* from which we get our word 'comfort', also means to strengthen. A good example of this can be found in the Bayeux tapestry, where Odo (William the Conqueror's brother) is said to be 'comforting' the troops by wielding a large mace above their heads. This seems to be the kind of comfort God offers Jesus in the garden – not an ability to feel better, but to look with a surer, clearer eye at what is to come … and to do it anyway.

God did not give Jesus what he wanted in this prayer but he did provide him with the strength to carry on. This is important for us to remember. It is very easy to assume that 'answered prayer' equates exactly with God giving us what we want and are asking for. This did not happen with Jesus, and may well not happen with us either. What God did provide was the strength to face the task in all its difficulty, not the ability to avoid it.

The Arrest

Matthew 26.47–56; Mark 14.43–52; Luke 22.47–54

> **Mark 14.43–52** Immediately, while he was still speaking, Judas, one of the twelve, arrived; and with him there was a crowd with swords and clubs, from the chief priests, the scribes, and the elders. [44]Now the betrayer had given them a sign, saying, 'The one I will kiss is the man; arrest him and lead him away under guard.' [45]So when he came, he went up to him at once and said, 'Rabbi!' and kissed him. [46]Then they laid hands on him and arrested him.
>
> [47]But one of those who stood near drew his sword and struck the slave of the high priest, cutting off his ear. [48]Then Jesus said to them, 'Have you come out with swords and clubs to arrest me as though I were a bandit? [49]Day after day I was with you in the temple teaching, and you did not arrest me. But let the scriptures be fulfilled.' [50]All of them deserted him and fled.
>
> [51]A certain young man was following him, wearing nothing but a linen cloth. They caught hold of him, [52]but he left the linen cloth and ran off naked.'

In John's Gospel Judas' departure from the meal is recorded (he went out into the night, 13.30), but in the other Gospels the first we know of Judas' absence is his return here with a crowd from the Sanhedrin.

> ## The Sanhedrin
>
> The word 'sanhedrin' literally means 'council' (and is translated as council in the NRSV). Since the Sanhedrin plays a key role in what is to follow it is helpful to attempt to identify it here. The Sanhedrin was founded around 200 years before the time of Jesus and was the ruling body of Judaism during the Hasmonean and Roman periods. However, since there are varying portrayals of the Sanhedrin in the literature of the time, scholars do not

agree about its scope of influence. Josephus described it as a political and legal body, whereas the Talmud saw it more as a solely religious body. In the Gospels it hovers between the two: the reasons for Jesus being brought before the Sanhedrin were religious but their ruling was political and legal. Scholars still do not agree about whether the Sanhedrin had the authority to condemn Jesus to death or not, but what happened does seem likely – that the Sanhedrin found Jesus guilty but then found the need to ask the Roman authorities to carry out the death penalty for them.

The Synoptic Gospels describe three groups who made up the Sanhedrin: the chief priests, the scribes and the elders. Sometimes all three of these are mentioned together; sometimes only two of the three groups are mentioned. At the arrest the three groups are mentioned and so imply that Jesus' arrest is sanctioned by the Sanhedrin itself. It is worth being alert to the mention of these groups since their inclusion in the narrative is often a quiet indication of the presence of the Sanhedrin.

The gesture of the kiss – which has become a widely accepted symbol of betrayal – appears in Mark to be merely a pragmatic means of identifying Jesus but might actually have even less significance than this. It was commonplace for Rabbis to greet their disciples with a kiss, and vice versa. It would be usual for Judas to greet his Rabbi with a kiss and would therefore be an obvious way to identify who among the group in the garden was, in fact, the Rabbi and leader of the disciples.

Matthew and Mark identify those who have come to arrest Jesus simply as 'a crowd', though the fact that this crowd includes one of the slaves of the high priest suggests that it was a crowd officially sanctioned by the Sanhedrin. Both Luke and John make the arresting crowd much more official. Luke indicates that the chief priests and the elders were themselves present along with, not the scribes, but the temple police (22.52). John added to the temple police a detachment of Roman soldiers (18.3). The problem of

Luke's inclusion of the chief priests and elders to the crowd is that their presence negates the necessity for the kiss – since they knew exactly who Jesus was.

All four Gospels include the cutting off of the ear of the slave of the High Priest. In the three Synoptic Gospels the slave is unnamed as is the person wielding the sword; only John's Gospel identifies the person cutting off the ear as Simon Peter and the slave as Malchus (but since he doesn't further identify who Malchus was, his name is, to us at least, of little value). It seems an odd and slightly random action to lash out with a sword and maim a servant standing by.

What part of the body?

The English translations all render the part of the body cut off as the ear but Mark and John use the double diminutive Greek word ōtarion (Mark 14.47, John 18.10); Matthew and Luke use simple diminutive ōtion (Matthew 26.51, Luke 22.51; though in the verse before, 22.50, Luke also used the more usual word for ear, ous). The use of the diminutive has led Raymond Brown among others to suggest that what was cut off was the earlobe or the outer edge of the ear rather than the whole ear, a suggestion which makes a lot of sense.

One possibility is that this is not 'a' slave but 'the' slave of the High Priest (the Greek certainly says so). If that is the case 'the' slave might have been the one leading the whole arresting party, not an insignificant bystander to the main action as some assume. This would mean that the person lashing out could then have thought that they were trying to save Jesus from arrest and was attempting to defend him. Of course the irony of the action is that lashing out with a sword is exactly the kind of thing a group of bandits might do, thus demonstrating to those who had come that the arrest was well-founded after all.

It is also worth noting that some scholars would argue that the cutting off of the slave's ear was not a random lashing out but the opening salvo of an armed rebellion of freedom fighters who had thought that Jesus had come to lead them in battle against the Romans. While this is possible, and would certainly explain the presence of the sword, little is made of it in the Gospels and it was at best a short-lived attempt at rebellion before the disciples all fled.

Luke's Gospel is the only Gospel that ends the account with Jesus healing the slave by touching his ear, though it is unclear whether the touch reattached the severed flesh or simply staunched the blood. The purpose of this narrative is to demonstrate that even at the time of his greatest crisis, Jesus revealed himself to be the kind of Son of God who never stopped caring for and nurturing those around him when they needed it.

Probably the best loved vignette of this whole scene is that of the young man running away naked from Gethsemane. Theories about who he was abound and, while it is probable that he was known to Mark's audience, it is impossible today to identify him with any certainty (or to explain why he was so oddly dressed). The romantic explanation that it was Mark himself can neither be proved nor disproved and it must be left to each of us to decide how likely it is. What this small vignette does provide, however, is a sense of the despair and horror of the moment. We need to remind ourselves of the deep and profound shame of nakedness within Judaism and then to recognize that the young man preferred this level of shame of running from the scene naked to the horror of being identified with Jesus. In the space of a few moments, Jesus was left utterly alone and those with him chose the worst kind of shame over any kind of association with him.

* * *

Reflection

Some artwork so captures a biblical scene that it is very difficult to see that scene in your mind without the iconic picture overlaying it. In this scene the picture that does this is the *Taking of*

Jesus by Caravaggio. It is classic Caravaggio. The background is dark and the central focus is of Judas kissing a hesitant and anxious Jesus. From one side of the painting armoured soldiers move in to capture Jesus, with a bystander peering over their shoulders, while to the other side someone rushes off, their arms raised in fear. The painting communicates turmoil, anxiety and terror but in my mind the overwhelming sense I get is one of shadows and darkness. All sorts of activity is taking place in front of our eyes, but off to the edges this activity fades into darkness and gloom and, as we look, it is almost as if the shadows are moving in.

This is certainly how Mark's account feels. The shadow of the cross has fallen over the whole Gospel but now we move from daylight, with a shadow falling across it, to twilight. This is no long summer twilight but a Middle Eastern one that goes from day to night in minutes. The daylight of Jesus' ministry has passed and night has fallen. The disciples who basked in the daylight of Jesus can barely be seen as they flee into the shadows of the night, and if you strain you can just catch a glimpse of a young man running naked through the trees in his effort to get away.

The Trials

Of all the episodes in the Passion narratives, the trials are the most difficult to tie with any certainty to history. The problem is that the only people present are Jesus and his opponents. As a result, exactly what happened has often been questioned by scholars. This book has not concerned itself with questions of proving historicity and it is not about to start now. It is worth noting, however, that we do know of two members of the Sanhedrin, Joseph of Arimathea and Nicodemus, who were sympathetic to Jesus and his cause. It is just possible that they recounted what went on, following Jesus' death and resurrection.

The trials are some of the most complex of the accounts of Jesus' Passion and the confusion felt by all those involved certainly communicates itself to the reader. At this point Jesus is passed around from authority to authority with the reasons for his death, both fabricated and real, trailing behind him as he went.

The High Priest/chief priests

One of the questions that arises when exploring the whole of the Gospels, but really comes to the fore here, is who the chief priests were. There is only one High Priest in office at any one time. His particular religious function was that he was the only one allowed in the Holy of Holies on the Day of Atonement (and only once in the year) to sprinkle the blood of the sin offering and burn incense. During the time of Jesus the High Priest also was the leader of the Sanhedrin and, to a certain extent, therefore a leader also of the people of Judea.

The chief priests, therefore, have no technical religious or political function but may well be an informal gathering of former high priests with authority granted to them as a result of this. One important feature of this era is the dominance of Annas' family among the high priests. Annas was appointed as the first High Priest after Herod Archelaus was deposed at the request of the Judeans in AD 6. Annas himself was then deposed as High Priest in AD 15 as a result of imposing death penalties that he had no authority to impose, but maintained a strong influence because his five sons and one son-in-law were high priests after him.

Annas, his sons and son-in-law and their dates as high priests

Annas ben Seth (AD 6–15).

Eleazar ben Ananus (AD 16–17).

Joseph ben Caiaphas (AD 18–36 AD), who had married the daughter of Annas.

Jonathan ben Ananus (AD 36–37 and 44).

Theophilus ben Ananus (AD 37–41).

Matthias ben Ananus (AD 43).

Ananus ben Ananus (AD 63).

These dates go way beyond the time of Jesus but illustrate Annas' family influence among the high priests for much of the first century. For many years during Jesus' life, Caiaphas, Annas' son-in-law, was High Priest, but this level of influence explains the role of Annas in this whole story and why, although not being High Priest, he was clearly still important.

The First Trial Before the Sanhedrin and the Mocking of Jesus

Matthew 26.59–68, Mark 14.55–65, Luke 22.63–71

Mark 14.55–65 Now the chief priests and the whole council were looking for testimony against Jesus to put him to death; but they found none. [56]For many gave false testimony against him, and their testimony did not agree. [57]Some stood up and gave false testimony against him, saying, [58]'We heard him say, "I will destroy this temple that is made with hands, and in three days I

---

will build another, not made with hands."' ⁵⁹But even on this point their testimony did not agree.

⁶⁰Then the high priest stood up before them and asked Jesus, 'Have you no answer? What is it that they testify against you?' ⁶¹But he was silent and did not answer. Again the high priest asked him, 'Are you the Messiah, the Son of the Blessed One?' ⁶²Jesus said, 'I am; and

"you will see the Son of Man seated at the right hand of the Power",

and "coming with the clouds of heaven."'

⁶³Then the high priest tore his clothes and said, 'Why do we still need witnesses? ⁶⁴You have heard his blasphemy! What is your decision?' All of them condemned him as deserving death. ⁶⁵Some began to spit on him, to blindfold him, and to strike him, saying to him, 'Prophesy!' The guards also took him over and beat him.

One of the big questions often asked of this part of the trial of Jesus is where this meeting of the Sanhedrin took place. The implication of Mark, which is stated clearly in Matthew and Luke, is that the Sanhedrin had been called together for an emergency meeting in the High Priest's house.

- **Matthew 26.57** 'Those who had arrested Jesus took him to Caiaphas the high priest, in whose house the scribes and the elders had gathered.'
- **Mark 14.53** 'They took Jesus to the high priest; and all the chief priests, the elders, and the scribes were assembled.'
- **Luke 22.54** 'Then they seized him and led him away, bringing him into the high priest's house. But Peter was following at a distance.'

The problem with this is that the Sanhedrin tractate of the Mishnah states clearly that capital trials must

- take place during the daytime
- not be held on the eve of a festival
- be held in one of three specified locations (which did not include the High Priest's house)
- not reach a conclusion on the same day as hearing evidence.

All of this somewhat undermines Jesus' trial here. Two points need to be raised in response. The first is that these regulations appear to reflect a later time than the time of Jesus, and whether they were, in fact, in place in the first century is unclear. Even more important is the question of whether this is a trial. We call it a trial but it has more of the hallmarks of a hurried exploration by the Sanhedrin about whether they feel justified in handing Jesus over to the Romans or not. In that case, they do not need to follow the rules of a capital trial. If the Sanhedrin rules were in place in the first century then it is possible that the Gospel writers are signalling to their audience that this is clearly not a capital trial because it takes place at night, during Passover, in the High Priest's house, with the verdict declared immediately.

The timing of the trial of Jesus

Matthew, Mark and John all have the first trial with the Sanhedrin/High Priest during the night and Jesus then being sent to Pilate first thing in the morning. Luke, in contrast, holds Jesus in the courtyard overnight and has all the trials the next day. This is probably, however, so that he could get the dramatic moment of Peter and Jesus in the courtyard together for Peter's denial (see below). It certainly seems likely that they would have tried Jesus as quickly as possible following his arrest, though the problems of this being the first solemn eve of Passover remain (see discussion above pp. 40–1).

Another issue that arises from this first 'trial' are the accusations levelled against Jesus. There are two noted in Matthew and Mark which become just one in Luke. Matthew's and Mark's accounts contain both the accusation that Jesus said he would destroy the temple and the question of whether Jesus considers himself to be the Messiah. It is this second accusation that is in Luke. The implication of Mark's Gospel is that there were many accusations against Jesus. This is very likely given the increasing conflict between him and the Jewish authorities in the last week of his life. The problem was that they were seeking grounds to kill him and none of the other accusations would have provided this.

Clearly the accusation of claiming to be the Messiah is the crucial one – and indeed the one that causes the High Priest to declare that Jesus has blasphemed. So important is it that Luke does not bother to record any other accusations. The question is what was it that Jesus said that triggered the claim of blasphemy? It is widely agreed by scholars that simply claiming to be the Messiah was not enough to trigger an accusation of blasphemy. There were a number of other people who made a similar claim around this time and they were not denounced by the Jewish authorities. It is much more likely that it is what Jesus said following the Messianic question that is key here.

So it was not Jesus' acceptance of the label 'Messiah', but that he said, 'you will see the Son of Man seated at the right hand of the Power', and 'coming with the clouds of heaven' (Mark 14.62). The thought of sitting anywhere in heaven let alone on his throne at God's right hand is a radical one. Jewish literature written in the Second Temple period hardly ever presents anyone being able to do this (the rare exceptions being Moses and Enoch). Sitting on the throne implies that the person described would be acting as ruler and judge. To describe someone doing this would have been radical, to claim that you would do it yourself, incendiary. It is almost certainly this claim that warranted the charge of blasphemy and gave the authorities the weighty accusation they needed to confirm the necessity for Jesus' death. (For a full discussion of this important point see Daniel Bock's excellent book *Blasphemy and Exaltation in Judaism: The Charge Against Jesus in Mark 14.53–65*, Baker Academic, 2000.)

The Trial of Peter

Matthew 26.58, 69–75; Mark 14.54, 66–72; Luke 22.54–60

> **Mark 14.54, 66–72** Peter had followed him at a distance, right into the courtyard of the high priest; and he was sitting with the guards, warming himself at the fire ... ⁶⁶While Peter was below in the courtyard, one of the servant-girls of the high priest came by. ⁶⁷When she saw Peter warming himself, she stared at him and said, 'You also were with Jesus, the man from Nazareth.' ⁶⁸But he denied it, saying, 'I do not know or understand what you are talking about.' And he went out into the forecourt. Then the cock crowed. ⁶⁹And the servant-girl, on seeing him, began again to say to the bystanders, 'This man is one of them.' ⁷⁰But again he denied it. Then after a little while the bystanders again said to Peter, 'Certainly you are one of them; for you are a Galilean.' ⁷¹But he began to curse, and he swore an oath, 'I do not know this man you are talking about.' ⁷²At that moment the cock crowed for the second time. Then Peter remembered that Jesus had said to him, 'Before the cock crows twice, you will deny me three times.' And he broke down and wept.

The way in which Peter's encounter with his accusers in the court-yard of the High Priest's house is interwoven with Jesus' trials indicates that we have here the contrast of two people under pressure. In Jesus' trial before the Sanhedrin, Jesus is challenged to answer the question of who he is; Peter in contrast is simply asked to confirm who he associates with. The contrast between the two episodes is striking.

Peter's denial gets greater as the questioning goes on. It began with a private conversation between him and a slave girl. The second time it was a public repudiation to both the slave girl and the bystanders. The third time, still publicly, he swore an oath that he did not know who Jesus was.

Luke emphasizes the contrast between Jesus' and Peter's trials even more by making Peter's trial the first thing to happen after

Jesus' arrest. It causes us to think back to Jesus' words to Peter in the previous scene where Jesus advised his disciples to pray that they might not come to a time of trial. They do not. Instead they fall asleep. What happens to Peter illustrates why it was so important that they did pray that they might not be brought to a time of trial – because when you are you may not respond as you hope that you will. Straight after Jesus' arrest Peter was brought to a time of trial and to his great distress he failed.

Luke emphasizes the level of Peter's failure by extending the period between each denial. In Mark the first two denials come close together, with a pause only between the second and third denial. In Luke there is a gap between each denial (and about an hour between the second and third one) which gives Peter time to think about it. This makes his denial more overtly deliberate and not just the result of the heat of the moment.

This betrayal is worse yet again in Luke because Jesus was in the courtyard with Peter while he denied him. In Matthew and Mark Jesus was inside the house on trial before the Sanhedrin while Peter denied him. In Luke, because Jesus' trial did not begin until the next morning, Jesus was waiting in the courtyard and so witnessed Peter's denial. Possibly the most heart-wrenching moment of the whole account occurs at the end of Peter's three denials when Jesus turned and looked at Peter, indicating that he had heard exactly what Peter had said (Luke 22.61). In Luke Peter denied Jesus not behind his back but in his presence.

There are varying traditions in the Gospels about how often the cock crowed around Peter's denial. In Matthew, Luke and John the cock crowed once and in Mark it crowed twice. The detail is of little significance; what is important is that Peter denied Jesus the very same night that he swore he would never leave him.

We are used to calling Peter's denial a denial of Jesus, which of course it was, but it was also a denial of who Peter was too. Peter had spent a lot of time in the presence of Jesus, had followed him with passion (if not entire understanding) and had committed himself to all that Jesus was. The real tragedy of Peter's denial was that, driven by fear, he turned his back on who he really was. No wonder his tears were tinged with such bitterness.

Judas' Change of Heart

Matthew 27.1–10

Matthew 27.1-10   When morning came, all the chief priests and the elders of the people conferred together against Jesus in order to bring about his death. [2]They bound him, led him away, and handed him over to Pilate the governor.

[3]When Judas, his betrayer, saw that Jesus was condemned, he repented and brought back the thirty pieces of silver to the chief priests and the elders. [4]He said, 'I have sinned by betraying innocent blood.' But they said, 'What is that to us? See to it yourself.'

[5]Throwing down the pieces of silver in the temple, he departed; and he went and hanged himself. [6]But the chief priests, taking the pieces of silver, said, 'It is not lawful to put them into the treasury, since they are blood money.' [7]After conferring together, they used them to buy the potter's field as a place to bury foreigners. [8]For this reason that field has been called the Field of Blood to this day.

[9]Then was fulfilled what had been spoken through the prophet Jeremiah, 'And they took the thirty pieces of silver, the price of the one on whom a price had been set, on whom some of the people of Israel had set a price, [10]and they gave them for the potter's field, as the Lord commanded me.'

Matthew's Gospel is the only Gospel which attempts some mitigation for Judas' actions. Acts contains a parallel account in which a Field of Blood was also bought with the proceeds of Judas' betrayal but this time by Judas himself, not by the authorities to whom he attempted to return the money. Acts also records his death but there the death is accidental (or a divine punishment for what he did) rather than as in Matthew as an act of remorse.

Acts 1.16–19 'Friends, the scripture had to be fulfilled, which the Holy Spirit through David foretold concerning Judas, who became a guide for those who arrested Jesus – [17]for he was numbered among us and was allotted his share in this ministry.' [18](Now this man acquired a field with the reward of his wickedness; and falling headlong, he burst open in the middle and all his bowels gushed out. [19]This became known to all the residents of Jerusalem, so that the field was called in their language Hakeldama, that is, Field of Blood.)

Matthew's Gospel certainly suggests that Judas had no idea that Jesus would be condemned to death. Indeed it is Matthew's Gospel that hints at the possibility that Judas hadn't intended Jesus to be punished in any way which is what sows the seed for some to wonder whether Judas was attempting to achieve reconciliation between the chief priests and Jesus: 'When Judas ... saw that he was condemned, he repented ...' (Matthew 27.3).

The more sympathetic reading offered by Matthew suggests that Judas' greatest crime was not waiting for forgiveness. The accounts of Jesus' arrest indicate that Judas may have been the only person to hand Jesus over, but he was not the only one to betray Jesus. John 21 is very clear about the reconciliation that was needed and which took place between Jesus and Peter. I have often wondered whether similar forgiveness would have been on offer for Judas had he been alive to receive it. Instead, overcome by remorse he gave up on God's forgiveness and hung himself.

The Trial Before Pilate

Matthew 27.11–25; Mark 15.1–15; Luke 23.1–7, 13–25

Mark 15.1–15   As soon as it was morning, the chief priests held a consultation with the elders and scribes and the whole council. They bound Jesus, led him away, and handed him over to Pilate. [2]Pilate asked him, 'Are you the King of the Jews?' He answered him, 'You say so.' [3]Then the chief priests accused him of many things. [4]Pilate asked him again, 'Have you no answer? See how many charges they bring against you.' [5]But Jesus made no further reply, so that Pilate was amazed.

[6]Now at the festival he used to release a prisoner for them, anyone for whom they asked. [7]Now a man called Barabbas was in prison with the rebels who had committed murder during the insurrection. [8]So the crowd came and began to ask Pilate to do for them according to his custom. [9]Then he answered them, 'Do you want me to release for you the King of the Jews?' [10]For he realized that it was out of jealousy that the chief priests had handed him over. [11]But the chief priests stirred up the crowd to have him release Barabbas for them instead.

[12]Pilate spoke to them again, 'Then what do you wish me to do with the man you call the King of the Jews?' [13]They shouted back, 'Crucify him!' [14]Pilate asked them, 'Why, what evil has he done?' But they shouted all the more, 'Crucify him!' [15]So Pilate, wishing to satisfy the crowd, released Barabbas for them; and after flogging Jesus, he handed him over to be crucified.

The first thing to notice about the trial before Pilate is that the chief priests accused Jesus of many things in 15.3. Again this hints at other accusations raised against Jesus of which we are told nothing. The key accusation before Pilate is, inevitably, different from the one before the Sanhedrin. The accusation here suggests treason. Claiming kingship in a Roman province entails an undermining of the Roman rule of law (ironically something that many Jews of the period would have been keen to do) but in this instance the charge is designed to require the Roman death penalty.

Pontius Pilate

In AD 6 the Judeans asked the Romans to depose the hated Archelaus. The events surrounding this can help to explain the nervousness of both the Romans and the Jewish authorities about riots at this time of year. The key incident in Archelaus' downfall was his refusal to listen to the people of Judea's request that he punish Herod the Great's advisers whom they regarded as responsible for various abuses of power including the martyrdom of two Pharisaic leaders. The ensuing riot that took place in the temple courts was put down by Archelaus' soldiers on the eve of Passover and resulted in the massacre of 3,000 people.

The people asked that he be deposed and from then on Judea was run as part of a larger Roman province (called Iudaea) which included Samaria and Idumea. The province was ruled by a Roman prefect, the fifth of whom was Pontius Pilate who ruled in AD 26–36.

Although Pilate is portrayed as conciliatory in the Gospel accounts, he was heavily criticized by both Philo and Josephus for his insensitivity towards the Jews and ultimately was recalled to Rome as a result of his harsh punishment of an uprising in Samaria. He may appear to be sensitive to the Jews in the Gospels but this appears to be a historical anomaly.

The tradition about freeing prisoners during a feast is one that is not attested anywhere outside the Gospels. It did happen from time to time but never on any regular basis that has been recorded elsewhere. As a result this can probably be interpreted as an attempt by Pilate to avoid killing Jesus whose guilt he doubted.

The key feature of Barabbas is that he was imprisoned with people who had been involved with an insurrection. Although Barabbas is not said explicitly to have been a rebel himself, the fact that he was imprisoned with rebels certainly suggests some

involvement. Jesus was subsequently crucified between two bandits (*lēstai*) and again the implication is that they were two rebels
from the same insurrection. The key feature of the *lēstai* is that the
word refers to politically motivated bandits who sought to drive
the Romans from Judea, with Jesus being placed by the Romans
alongside those who really wanted to overthrow their rule. The
question is clearly whether the crowd would recognize Jesus as
deserving death alongside those who clearly warranted it (in the
minds of the Romans at least).

The two Gospels that go furthest in attempting to exonerate Pilate's role in Jesus' death are John and Matthew. In John's
Gospel this takes the form of Pilate stating three times that he
found no case against Jesus (18.38; 19.4, 6). In Matthew the por-
trayal is more complex and adds some details to the narrative in
27.19 and 24 which are worth exploring here:

- **Matthew 27.19**   While he was sitting on the judgment seat, his
  wife sent word to him, 'Have nothing to do with that innocent
  man, for today I have suffered a great deal because of a dream
  about him.'
- **Matthew 27.24**   So when Pilate saw that he could do nothing,
  but rather that a riot was beginning, he took some water and
  washed his hands before the crowd, saying, 'I am innocent of
  this man's blood; see to it yourselves.'

The two episodes appear connected to each other. It is slightly
unfortunate that the NRSV uses the word 'innocent' in both
verses since the word translates different Greek words each
time. Pilate's wife declared Jesus to be *dikaios* which means law
abiding, upright or respectable in a Roman context and just
or righteous in a more religious setting (a resonance which is
almost certainly intended by Matthew). Jesus was both a model
Roman citizen and a man righteous before God. In verse 24
Pilate declared himself to be *athōos* which is more guiltless than
anything else.

The wording used by Pilate's wife is significant. When translated
literally it reads '... nothing to you and to that upright/righteous

man' and was a structure that is also used in 8.29 when the demoniacs ask Jesus 'what to us and to you?' A similar structure is also used famously in John 2.4 when Jesus said to his mother 'Woman, what to you and to me?' In all of these settings the point of the construction is the questioning of a connection between the two parties. In other words Pilate's wife was saying this has nothing to do with you, do not get involved. Pilate's declaration in verse 24 suggests that he half listened to his wife. One suspects that she meant don't get involved at all, not let them have their own way and then declare yourself innocent of what happened.

The *bēma*

In both Matthew and John's Gospel, Pilate sat down on the judgement seat to declare his sentencing of Jesus. The Greek word for judgement seat is *bēma*.

The *bēma* is literally a step, but was in Roman contexts to be the place from which official pronouncements were made. So, for example, Paul was brought to the *bēma* on which Gallio sat for judgement in Acts 18.12 and again to the *bēma* that Festus sat on in Acts 25.6. The *bēma* clearly symbolized justice within the Roman world since Acts reports with horror that the leader of the synagogue in Ephesus was beaten before the *bēma* in Acts 18.17 and Gallio did nothing. The 'seat' appears to have been outside in all these locations and was therefore the public place from which official judgements were pronounced. The fact that Pilate's wife sent a note to the *bēma* suggests that hers was a last-minute intervention into a judgement already made.

Pilate subsequently in Matthew's Gospel returned to the praetorium (translated by the NRSV as the governor's headquarters). The Roman prefect's headquarters would have been in Caesarea; the praetorium in Jerusalem was probably the place he came just for festivals or times of potential trouble (or both!). It probably mixed private accommodation for the prefect and his family with barracks for the soldiers. This is certainly suggested by Matthew 27.27 and Mark 15.16: when the soldiers gather to mock Jesus

> they do so in the praetorium which suggests it is their natural place to go.

The people's response to Pilate's attempt to avoid culpability for Jesus' death is to claim responsibility for themselves: 'Then the people as a whole answered, "His blood be on us and on our children!"' (Matthew 27.25). This verse has had one of the most repulsive afterlives of all the verses in the Bible. Matthew 27.25 has over the centuries been used to justify awful levels of anti-Semitism, on the grounds that if the people claim culpability for themselves and their children then they could legitimately be punished for it hundreds, even thousands, of years later.

It is hard to imagine that this is what Matthew meant here. He, like the other Gospel writers, has already presented us with a wide range of people who could be considered to be culpable of Jesus' death (from Judas to the Jewish authorities; from Peter to Pilate). The acceptance of responsibility should not be seen as guilt but that, unlike Pilate, they were prepared to accept their role in what was going on. It is also unlikely that 'children' means 'children's children's children's children' and so on. 'Our children' refers to one generation, the one following those present at Jesus' death. If any punishment was seen to befall them for their role in Jesus' crucifixion, the fall of Jerusalem would be the most likely event and is a theme that can also be found in Luke's Gospel.

The crowd

Anyone who has attended a dramatic or semi-dramatic reading of the Passion narrative will at some point have had to play the part of the crowd calling out 'crucify him, crucify him'. Every time I do this, it reminds me how easy it is to become complicit in something without thinking it through particularly well, especially in a group.

In Mark's Gospel three different groups respond in stereo-typical ways to Jesus. The authorities are always antagonistic, the disciples nearly always miss the point of what Jesus says and the crowd is often amazed. The reaction of the crowd, then, reminds us of what a fine line there is between amazement and condemnation. The crowd, it seems, saw Jesus as an intriguing, external fascination and it took very little time for them to turn from amazement to dismissal.

What might it have felt like to be in the middle of the crowd and unsure? How easy might it have been to turn the crowd, to change their minds? Impossible questions to answer, but every time I am called upon to shout 'crucify, crucify' the questions return – and that is why it is such a powerful thing to do.

The Exchange Between Jesus and Pilate in John's Gospel

John 18.28—19.16a

John's Gospel contains a number of details that have made their way firmly into the popular imagination of what went on, for example, the fact that the Jewish leaders would not enter the praetorium for purity reasons (18.28) and that they also explicitly stated that they were not allowed to condemn anyone to death (18.31). In John the focus, however, is the long conversation between Pilate and Jesus which eclipses all other encounters so that we discover little about the conversation between Jesus and the Sanhedrin (which is cast as two episodes, one with Annas and the other with Caiaphas, Annas' son-in-law and the High Priest).

In great contrast Jesus' encounter with Pilate has huge drama (and many more verses than the other Gospels). Raymond Brown observes in his wonderful commentary on John that the scene falls into seven episodes.

1 **18.28–32**   Outside: The Jews demand Jesus' death.
2 **18.33–38a**   Inside: Pilate talks with Jesus about truth.
3 **18.38b–40**   Outside: Pilate finds no case against Jesus and introduces Barabbas.
4 **19.1–3**   Inside: Soldiers beat Jesus.
5 **19.4–8**   Outside: Pilate finds no case against Jesus (again) and says 'Behold the Man'.
6 **19.9–11**   Inside: Pilate talks with Jesus about power.
7 **19.12–16a**   Outside: Pilate sits on the *bēma* and hands Jesus over to be killed.

The drama of the whole scene is exacerbated here with Pilate going in and out from the Jews to Jesus and back again. The two conversations inside – first about the nature of truth and second about the nature of power – focus sharply some of the contrasts John loves so well. Pilate whose job it was as judge to discern and declare truth was forced to ask Jesus what truth is. In a similar way he was the one with the power over Jesus and yet demonstrated himself to have very little power in the face of the one from whom true power flows. The all-powerful Roman ruler turned out not to have all that much power after all. As so often, the way in which John's Gospel tells the narrative helps us to see more truly what is really going on in the world. Here the person who was tasked to discern truth and exercise power, found himself utterly bewildered in the face of him who was truth and who knew that true power only exists when you give it up.

The Trial Before Herod Antipas

Luke 23.7–12

Luke 23.7–12   And when he learned that he was under Herod's jurisdiction, he sent him off to Herod, who was himself in Jerusalem at that time. [8]When Herod saw Jesus, he was very glad, for he had been wanting to see him for a long time, because he had heard about him and was hoping to see him perform some sign. [9]He questioned him at some length, but Jesus gave him no answer.

[10]The chief priests and the scribes stood by, vehemently accusing him. [11]Even Herod with his soldiers treated him with contempt and mocked him; then he put an elegant robe on him, and sent him back to Pilate.

[12]That same day Herod and Pilate became friends with each other; before this they had been enemies.

Luke's Gospel is alone in proposing another trial for Jesus with Herod Antipas. You can see how he made the connection but whether a third trial was really necessary is debatable.

After his death, Herod the Great's former territory was split into three: Archelaus ruled Judea, Antipas ruled Galilee, and Perea and Philip ruled Gaulanitis, Trachonitis, Batanæa and Paneas. As a result, Antipas was, technically, the ruler of the place where Jesus spent the vast majority of his ministry and he would have been in Jerusalem, like everyone else, for the Passover. He was a troublesome ruler, however, constantly asking the Romans to extend the territory he had been given (since Herod the Great had promised him the whole kingdom before his death but then changed his mind at the last minute). It is highly unlikely that he would have been deemed by the prefect to have had sufficient authority to be worth sending Jesus to.

* * *

Reflection

Although the different Gospels writers portray the trials of Jesus in slightly different ways, a similar feeling emerges from all of the Gospel accounts. Each of the key figures and groups became more and more frenetic as the trials progressed. The Jewish authorities were anxious, the crowd whipped up and baying for blood and Pilate appears bemused and apparently outmanoeuvred. In the centre of this maelstrom of emotion and anxiety, Jesus alone remained a still centre. So still in fact that he barely spoke. Alongside this Peter also reached his own time of trial and spoke out of and in response to the many emotions in the air.

This seems to suggest that the writer of Ecclesiastes was in fact right and there are times to speak and times to keep silence (Ecclesiastes 3.7). This seems to run contrary to a natural sense of what to do in such contexts. Surely when we are on trial the best thing to do is to defend ourselves? The answer given by Jesus' trial seems to be that times of trial are when we need all the wisdom available to us. Unless we are as wise as serpents we will find ourselves defeated, as Peter was, during times of trial. They are truly, as Jesus suggested to his disciples in Luke's Gospel, to be avoided at all costs because by definition they are times of testing – and we may not respond as we hope we will. Peter certainly didn't.

There are times when words are essential but also times when words will simply draw us into a spiralling dynamic of fear and bewilderment. By not speaking much during his trial, Jesus managed to remain outside the escalation of emotion that swirled around him. In contrast Peter did not and was sucked into a response that he deeply regretted. Jesus' trials do seem to have been a time for him to keep silence and to remain a still centre in the midst of chaos and fear.

On Trials

'Do not bring us to the time of trial ...'
But if being tested is unavoidable,
  Give us the courage to face it full on
  and not to shy away from what we fear might happen

  Give us the integrity to stay true to who you are
  and who we are

  Give us the wisdom to know when to speak
  and when to stay silent

  Give us the stillness to avoid
  being drawn into the maelstrom of other people's emotions

'Do not bring us to the time of trial ...'
But if being tested is unavoidable,
  Be with us and help us to face our trials
  with your courage, integrity, wisdom and stillness.

4

The Crucifixion

The Mocking of Jesus

Matthew 27.27–31; Mark 15.16–20; Luke 23.11; John 19.1–3

> **Mark 15.16–20** Then the soldiers led him into the courtyard of the palace (that is, the governor's headquarters); and they called together the whole cohort. [17]And they clothed him in a purple cloak; and after twisting some thorns into a crown, they put it on him. [18]And they began saluting him, 'Hail, King of the Jews!' [19]They struck his head with a reed, spat upon him, and knelt down in homage to him. [20]After mocking him, they stripped him of the purple cloak and put his own clothes on him. Then they led him out to crucify him.

Matthew, Mark and Luke all have an account of Jesus being mocked twice. On the first occasion Jesus is challenged to prophesy, on the second a mock enthronement ceremony takes place. There are some key differences, however, between John's and Luke's accounts which are worth noting:

- In John there is only one mocking and it takes place in the centre of the whole trial with Pilate just before Jesus is led outside (19.1–3).
- Luke's mockings are different from those in Matthew and Mark. The first takes place before any trial has happened at all (22.63–65) and the second during the trial with Herod (23.11).

- Matthew and Mark locate each – probably more sensibly – after each phase of the trial. So Jesus is mocked and called upon to prophesy after his encounter with the Sanhedrin (Matthew 26.66–68; Mark 14.65) and then ridiculed in a mock enthronement by the Roman soldiers (Matthew 27.27–31; Mark 15.16–20).

What these two incidents seem to illustrate is that we mock most what we fear most. After the Sanhedrin encounter they challenged Jesus to prophesy, since a true prophet who spoke God's words to his people was greatly to be feared; after Pilate's sentencing they ridiculed Jesus' kingship as the Romans feared true power the most. Of course this reminds us that our ability to mock something does not make it any less true. Jesus did speak the very words of God and was a king even though he was mocked for both.

Simon of Cyrene

Matthew 27.32; Mark 15.21; Luke 23.26

> **Mark 15.21** They compelled a passer-by, who was coming in from the country, to carry his cross; it was Simon of Cyrene, the father of Alexander and Rufus.

Most scholars now agree that the cross Jesus was called upon to carry was not the whole thing but the cross section which would be subsequently fitted into place on the upright which was already in place. The verb used to describe their action of compelling Simon to help is a technical word referring to the accepted custom in the Ancient world that an occupying soldier could compel a local citizen to help them carry a load or something similar. This custom is also referred to by Jesus in Matthew 5.41 where he advises his followers to carry the load an extra mile if a soldier insists on their help. Here Simon is forced to carry an unusual load; we are left to assume that this is because Jesus, weakened as he was from the flogging (Matthew 27.26; Mark 15.15), was unable to carry his cross the full distance.

Although Simon is declared as being from Cyrene (modern-day Libya), it is most likely that he was part of a Cyrenian Jewish community that lived in Jerusalem at the time. One small detail is intriguing. He is said to have come in from the country. The question is why he was coming in then. If the Synoptic timings are correct Passover had already started. We noted above that Jesus and his disciples did not go out as far as their usual lodging place in Bethany so that they could remain in the confines of the city for the festival. So where had Simon been and why was he returning now? Wherever it was, he must very quickly have regretted his ill-timed return.

Mark's Gospel offers us one more detail: the name of Simon's two sons. The only explanation for this is that the two sons, Alexander and Rufus, were known to Mark's community and the mentioning of their names helped Mark's readers to work out which Simon he was talking about. If this is the case then Simon's family and maybe also Simon himself were after Jesus' death followers of the Way. It may be that the action of carrying Jesus' cross had been the catalyst for Simon joining the community.

It is interesting to notice that John's Gospel appears to be clear that Jesus carried the cross by himself: 'So they took Jesus; and carrying the cross by himself, he went out to what is called The Place of the Skull, which in Hebrew is called Golgotha' (John 19.16–17). It is unclear how seriously we should take this. It could be a simple observation that Jesus carried his own cross or it could be an attempt to counter the Simon of Cyrene tradition.

While the Wood is Green

Luke 23.27–31

Matthew and Mark have Jesus arrive very quickly at the crucifixion site following the help of Simon of Cyrene, Luke on the other hand recounts a more detailed conversation during the journey to the place of execution between Jesus and the women of Jerusalem.

Luke 23.27–31   A great number of the people followed him, and among them were women who were beating their breasts and wailing for him. [28]But Jesus turned to them and said, 'Daughters of Jerusalem, do not weep for me, but weep for yourselves and for your children. [29]For the days are surely coming when they will say, "Blessed are the barren, and the wombs that never bore, and the breasts that never nursed." [30]Then they will begin to say to the mountains, "Fall on us"; and to the hills, "Cover us." [31] For if they do this when the wood is green, what will happen when it is dry?'

A number of times in the run-up to this point, Jesus has pointed attention beyond the catastrophe that is about to befall him towards the disaster coming towards Jerusalem in the future. This is yet another of those occasions. Jesus' comment here makes a direct link between what is happening to Jesus and what will happen to Jerusalem. The women should mourn for themselves, Jesus states, because the fall of the temple and the destruction of the city are as certain a fate as Jesus' own death in a few hours' time.

Most people take the 'they' in verse 31 to refer to those who are sending Jesus to his death. If they behave like this to him (when the wood is green) just imagine how great the conflagration will be when it is dry. While he might be referring just to the Jewish authorities, it is much more likely that he is referring to all the players in this drama, Romans included. If this is how they behave among themselves and to each other now, just imagine how great and terrible the outcome will be when attitudes have had time to harden, fear has had time to grow, and conflict to worsen. People's reactions to Jesus have demonstrated a deeply ingrained inability to recognize God in their midst, a profound reluctance to give up their determined grip on power and a refusal to turn and be transformed. Given these hardened attitudes, there is only one outcome possible. As a result, Jesus advises the women to begin mourning for themselves and their families because disaster is sure to come.

* * *

Reflection

I am not the only person to be intrigued by Simon of Cyrene. He gets far more attention than the single verse in which he is mentioned warrants, but it is Mark's account that draws our attention. As far as we know, Simon was entirely unconnected to Jesus until this moment. The accounts suggest that his journey 'from the field' was coincidental. He had been out of the city and bumped into the execution party on his way back. What intrigues me is that his family then seems to be known to Mark's community after this event.

When we think about the proclamation of the gospel it is often in terms of the gospel at its best. If we proclaim it really well, with all the skill available to us and present Christianity in its very best light, then perhaps people will be persuaded. Here something else seems to have happened. Simon encountered Jesus at one of the worst moments of Jesus' life. This was a very different first encounter to that, say, of Peter, who was called to follow Jesus and drawn to him by all he had to offer. Simon may have encountered Jesus at a terrible moment, but Mark's Gospel suggests that it was enough for his sons to be drawn in.

I am not for a moment suggesting that we should consciously and deliberately cultivate our worst selves as a missional strategy but it is, perhaps, worth reminding ourselves that it is not excellence that draws people to Christ, but Christ himself. Here Christ, battered, bruised and about to die, seems to have drawn to him someone whose whole life was changed as a result.

The Crucifixion: Part 1

Matthew 27.33–54; Mark 15.22–39; Luke 23.27–43; John 19.18–25a

One of the key features of the crucifixion narratives in all the Gospels is that in different ways the crucifixion draws together some of the strands that have been present throughout the telling of the whole of Jesus' life and ministry. It is worth paying attention to the themes that emerge in the telling of the crucifixion in each of the Gospels as it can offer an illustration of some of the key themes of that Gospel.

Mark 15.22-32 Then they brought Jesus to the place called Golgotha (which means the place of a skull). ²³And they offered him wine mixed with myrrh; but he did not take it.

²⁴And they crucified him, and divided his clothes among them, casting lots to decide what each should take. ²⁵It was nine o'clock in the morning when they crucified him. ²⁶The inscription of the charge against him read, 'The King of the Jews.' ²⁷And with him they crucified two bandits, one on his right and one on his left. ²⁹Those who passed by derided him, shaking their heads and saying, 'Aha! You who would destroy the temple and build it in three days, ³⁰save yourself, and come down from the cross!' ³¹In the same way the chief priests, along with the scribes, were also mocking him among themselves and saying, 'He saved others; he cannot save himself. ³²Let the Messiah, the King of Israel, come down from the cross now, so that we may see and believe.' Those who were crucified with him also taunted him.

The offering of wine

The offering of wine to Jesus is an important strand in all four Gospels, though its purpose is differently understood in the different Gospels.

In Luke and John's Gospel Jesus is offered wine once.

- **Luke 23.36–37**   The soldiers also mocked him, coming up and offering him sour wine, [37]and saying, 'If you are the King of the Jews, save yourself!'
- **John 19.29–30**   A jar full of sour wine was standing there. So they put a sponge full of the wine on a branch of hyssop and held it to his mouth. [30]When Jesus had received the wine, he said, 'It is finished.' Then he bowed his head and gave up his spirit.

Whereas in Matthew and Mark Jesus was offered wine twice.

- **Matthew 27.33–34**   And when they came to a place called Golgotha (which means Place of a Skull), [34]they offered him wine to drink, mixed with gall; but when he tasted it, he would not drink it.
- **Matthew 27.48**   At once one of them ran and got a sponge, filled it with sour wine, put it on a stick, and gave it to him to drink.

And

- **Mark 15.23**   And they offered him wine mixed with myrrh; but he did not take it.
- **Mark 15.36**   And someone ran, filled a sponge with sour wine, put it on a stick, and gave it to him to drink, saying, 'Wait, let us see whether Elijah will come to take him down.'

A brief glance at these different traditions indicates that Luke understood the offering of wine to be further mockery of Jesus, but John saw it as an act of compassion which allowed Jesus to die. The double tradition of the offering of wine in Matthew and Mark also picks up this strand of mockery and compassion, along with a new strand – curiosity.

The first wine offered to Jesus in Mark was laced with myrrh. This suggests that it was offered out of compassion. There is a tradition in the Talmud (Babylonian Sanhedrin 43a) which indicates that those being led out to execution should be offered wine laced with frankincense which would have had an anaesthetic effect (although myrrh is not mentioned here it is thought it would have had a similar effect to frankincense).

In contrast the tradition in Matthew states that the wine was mixed with 'gall'. This word can have a range of meanings but is associated with things that make the taste bitter. In this case it was an extension of the mocking of Jesus already begun by the soldiers: a king would expect fine wine served to him – deliberately bitter wine parodies what you would offer to a king. In both Matthew and Mark Jesus declined the wine at this point but this would be for different reasons: in Mark because he had accepted the 'cup' of suffering and intended to drink it as his Father asked; in Matthew because it was bitter and he refused the mocking offered.

The first giving of wine in Matthew and Mark should not be confused with the second. In both Matthew and Mark there is a hint that the second giving of wine was an action, if not of compassion, of curiosity. The wine he was offered here was simply sour wine with nothing added to it. Sour wine would have referred to a very cheap wine drunk regularly by Roman soldiers that would have had what some commentators call 'a bracing effect'. Jesus, just before this, cried out to someone that some bystanders think is Elijah. There is a suggestion that giving him wine to drink would revive him sufficiently for them to see either whether Elijah came or what he would say next. Its purpose being neither mockery nor compassion but curiosity. They were sufficiently interested in this dying man that they now wished to see what might happen next. As it happened, in both Matthew and Mark, Jesus then died straightaway so their curiosity was unassuaged despite offering him wine to drink.

Golgotha

Despite extensive discussion there is no definitive proof of the site of Jesus' crucifixion. The traditional place (now inside the Church of the Holy Sepulchre) could well be the spot where Jesus died but it would be impossible to prove it. The location would have been just outside the city walls, something that would have been vital given the bann on dead bodies within the city itself.

The four Gospels all associate the name of the place with the word 'skull'. This involves assuming that the word translated was in Aramaic *gulgultā*, a word which simply means 'skull'. If this is correct it could have got that name either because of its appearance or because it was the place where people were crucified. Some scholars, however, have wondered whether the Gospel writers were translating the wrong Aramaic word. A very similar sounding phrase *gol goatha* would mean in Aramaic 'mount of execution' and therefore be a description rather than a place name.

Somewhat intriguingly, if you take the name of the place from the gospel tradition (that it means place of the skull) there is no association with a hill. This tradition either came in from fourth-century pilgrim records or from the alternative meaning of Golgotha as mount of execution.

The word 'Calvary' comes from the Latin translation of 'place of the skull' (*Calvariae Locus*).

Casting lots for his clothes

All the Gospels have the episode of casting lots to divide Jesus' clothes but it is in John's Gospel that the episode takes on the greatest meaning. In Matthew, Mark and Luke the reference is simply to dividing Jesus' clothes equally between the soldiers in fulfilment of Psalm 22.18.

> **Psalm 22.18**   they divide my clothes among themselves, and for my clothing they cast lots.

John, however, understands the two halves of the verse to refer to a different action rather than the same action. The verse contains classic Hebrew parallelism (where the same thing is said twice in slightly different ways), but John understands this as referring to two actions, not just one.

> **John 19.23-24**   When the soldiers had crucified Jesus, they took his clothes and divided them into four parts, one for each soldier. They also took his tunic; now the tunic was seamless, woven in one piece from the top. [24]So they said to one another, 'Let us not tear it, but cast lots for it to see who will get it.' This was to fulfil what the scripture says, 'They divided my clothes among themselves, and for my clothing they cast lots.'

So they divided his outer garments between them and attempted to keep the inner garment, the tunic, in a single piece, and hence cast lots for it. Some scholars have suggested a theological significance in the not tearing of the tunic. An interesting suggestion is that it was seen by John as parallel to the ankle-length tunic of the high priest which is described as a single long woven cloth by Josephus in his history of the Jews (*Antiquities* III.7.4).

> **They do not know what they are doing**
>
> **Luke 23.34**   Then Jesus said, 'Father, forgive them; for they do not know what they are doing.'
>
> Luke's telling of the crucifixion narrative cleverly keeps our gaze fixed on the two points that Luke has by now brought to our attention: the interweaving of Jesus' fate with the fate of Jerusalem as

a whole. Just as in his conversation with the women of Jerusalem above, Jesus draws our attention in 23.24 to the fact that the people of his day are sleepwalking towards disaster and have no comprehension of what it is they are doing.

Yes they do need forgiveness for what they are doing to Jesus but that 'not knowing what they are doing' stretches much further than just Jesus' death. Not only do they not understand who Jesus is, they equally have no idea of the legacy they are laying down and the dire consequences to the city of Jerusalem that their 'not knowing what they are doing' are going to bring.

Jesus was right – they truly needed God's compassion and forgiveness.

The accusations

In Mark's Gospel the whole crucifixion scene is designed to continue the mocking and misunderstanding of Jesus first by the Romans and then by the passers-by (who included the Sanhedrin). While on the cross Jesus was ridiculed for being the 'King of Jews' by the inscribed title (15.26); for being a bandit by being crucified between two other bandits (15.27); for claiming to be able to destroy the temple (15.29); for being unable to come down from the cross and demonstrate his power as Messiah (15.30).

The irony for us is that we know that Jesus was the King of the Jews; that he was a 'bandit' insomuch as his power directly threatened and undermined Roman rule; that his death would ultimately end in the destruction of the temple and that had he chosen he could easily have come down from the cross. He was rightly and wrongly crucified for all these reasons and none of them. Rightly because he was King of the Jews, etc., but wrongly because this didn't mean what they thought it meant. Even at his moment of death those who had brought it about (both Romans and Jews) still entirely failed to understand who he was, what he had come for, or why he was dying.

Bandits/criminals

As we have noted above, the word used by Matthew and Mark for the people crucified one on either side of Jesus was *lēstēs*. This is more than just a 'robber' and is why the word is most often translated as bandit. These were political revolutionaries many of whom lived in the hill country of Galilee who stole property but did so to undermine the power of Roman rule.

In contrast to this, in Luke's Gospel the two are not called 'bandits' but 'criminals' (the Greek word is *kakourgos*, literally an evil-doer, 23.32). This defines them over against Jesus who is declared by the Centurion in Luke's Gospel to be 'innocent' or 'a just man' (the Greek word is *dikaios*). This allows Luke, therefore, to stress that Jesus was entirely undeserving of the fate that befell him.

This brings us back to the question from the introduction – Why did Jesus die? The answer seems to lie here: because everything he came to be and do was seen not as freedom but as threat. The real reason Jesus died was because his contemporaries – which at this point in Jesus' ministry tragically even included his own disciples – simply couldn't understand the freedom he had come to give. They saw what he offered as an encroachment on their own territory that needed resisting, rather than the gift that it was.

Mark 15.28

Older translations such as the King James version have an additional verse which you will not find in more modern translations. It is a quotation from Isaiah 53.12: 'And the scripture was fulfilled, which saith, And he was numbered with the transgressors.' Modern textual scholars agree that this verse was a later addition and can only be found in manuscripts of Mark's Gospel from a much later period. As a result modern translations omit it and leave verse 28 blank.

Save yourself

Mark's Gospel has the mocking of Jesus from three loose groups: passers-by, the chief priests and the scribes and the bandits crucified with him. In Luke's Gospel this mocking is more pointed and defined. Again three groups mocked him: the leaders, the soldiers and the criminals crucified with him but their words mirror each other much more clearly.

> **Luke 23.35-39** And the people stood by, watching; but the leaders scoffed at him, saying, 'He saved others; let him save himself if he is the Messiah of God, his chosen one!' [36]The soldiers also mocked him, coming up and offering him sour wine, [37]and saying, 'If you are the King of the Jews, save yourself!' [38]There was also an inscription over him, 'This is the King of the Jews.' [39]One of the criminals who were hanged there kept deriding him and saying, 'Are you not the Messiah? Save yourself and us!'

The key feature in Luke's Gospel is the three-times repeated call to Jesus to 'save himself'. This mocking, especially because it is Luke's Gospel, once more brings to mind the temptation narratives. As we have noted on a number of occasions already, the theme of temptation is a key one in Luke and recurs a number of times throughout the Gospel. Here it returns in the words of the soldiers to Jesus. 'If you are the King of the Jews' mimics the words of the devil in the temptations: 'If you are the Son of God' (4.3 and 4.9).

The taunting links Jesus' ability to save himself with his ability to save others and in doing so laces this temptation with irony. Luke knows, we know and Jesus knows that it is precisely his refusal to save himself that means that he can save us. Indeed this refusal to save himself is the demonstration of his 'kingship' par excellence. The taunting of Jesus simply confirms what he has stated already – that they do not know what they are doing.

* * *

Reflection

The ironic tragedy of Jesus' death was that he died for both the right and the wrong reasons. The reasons given both directly and indirectly in Mark's crucifixion narrative for his death: that he was King of the Jews; that he was a political revolutionary and that he would destroy the temple, were all to a certain extent true. He was the long-awaited King of the Jews; what he represented would undermine Roman political power and the temple was eventually destroyed, but he still died for the wrong reasons. The power he represented was a power unlike any experienced before or since. It was not enacted with violence or displays of military splendour but with love and self-sacrifice. Those in authority were right to fear Jesus' power since it was so much greater than their own but it was not manifested in ways they recognized. Indeed Jesus' power was at its greatest when his opponents believed him defeated. Hanging on the cross was the supreme moment when Jesus was revealed to be King, Revolutionary and Messiah. Jesus' opponents believed that power was strengthened by hanging on to it with all your might; Jesus revealed that true power was to be found in letting it go.

The Crucifixion: Part 2

Matthew 27.45–56; Mark 15.33–41; Luke 23.40–49;
John 19.25b–37

Mark 15.33–41   When it was noon, darkness came over the whole land until three in the afternoon. [34]At three o'clock Jesus cried out with a loud voice, 'Eloi, Eloi, lema sabachthani?' which means, 'My God, my God, why have you forsaken me?' [35]When some of the bystanders heard it, they said, 'Listen, he is calling for Elijah.' [36]And someone ran, filled a sponge with sour wine, put it on a stick, and gave it to him to drink, saying, 'Wait, let us see whether Elijah will come to take him down.' [37]Then Jesus gave a loud cry and breathed his last.

[38]And the curtain of the temple was torn in two, from top to bottom. [39]Now when the centurion, who stood facing him, saw that in this way he breathed his last, he said, 'Truly this man was God's Son!' [40]There were also women looking on from a distance; among them were Mary Magdalene, and Mary the mother of James the younger and of Joses, and Salome. [41]These used to follow him and provided for him when he was in Galilee; and there were many other women who had come up with him to Jerusalem.

Despair and hope

Jesus' cry of despair from the cross has formed the centre of much theological speculation about divine self-abandonment and its significance for our understanding of the Trinity. Such speculation takes this part of Matthew's and Mark's Gospels as a springboard into further reflection. In what I am about to say and explore I do not intend for a moment to undermine these kinds of important theological speculations, but simply to point to something that is going on in and behind the text which an overconcentration on verse 34 can easily miss.

Darkness

Matthew, Mark and Luke (but not John) all recount that Jesus' time on the cross was accompanied by a deep darkness over the whole land. It is clear that this darkness symbolized something about Jesus' death, the question is, what was it? It is not clear whether the darkness was caused by a full solar eclipse or simply by heavy storm clouds but it seems likely that the darkness was seen as an early fulfilment of Matthew 24.29.

Matthew 24.29 'Immediately after the suffering of those days the sun will be darkened, and the moon will not give its light; the stars will fall from heaven, and the powers of heaven will be shaken.'

As is very clear, Jesus' cry from the cross is not made in his own original words but by quoting the first verse of Psalm 22. It is important to recognize that this is not the only part of Psalm 22 behind this part of the text. It is striking to observe the following verses as well.

- **22.7**   All who see me mock at me; they make mouths at me, they shake their heads ...
- **22.17–18**   They stare and gloat over me; they divide my clothes among themselves, and for my clothing they cast lots.

This seems to indicate that Mark, if not also Jesus, observed strong resonances between the psalm and what was happening to Jesus on the cross. The question is then raised about how far through the psalm we are meant to read at this point.

Eloi, Eloi Lema Sabachtani

It is important to notice that Jesus' cry from the cross is in Aramaic. Even Matthew's altered cry 'Eli, Eli, lema sabachthani?' (Matthew 27.46) is also in Aramaic since Eli is an alternative to Eloi in Aramaic. This raises the question of what significance we are to put on Jesus' quoting from the scriptures in Aramaic not Hebrew. Although Aramaic was the language Jesus would have spoken every day, Hebrew remained the sacred language. Nevertheless there are numerous editions of the Hebrew scriptures in Aramaic from around this time and earlier which suggests that certain people would have known the scriptures in Aramaic.

Since Aramaic was Jesus' mother tongue it may explain why he used it to quote scriptures close to his death.

It was common within Judaism to use the first word or line of something to imply the whole. This is particularly true of the names of the books of the Old Testament, which are all called after the first word they contain. So for example the book of Genesis is called Bereshit which is Hebrew for 'In the Beginning', the first word of Genesis 1.1. The word Bereshit is not meant just to refer to itself but to the whole book. This raises the possibility that when Jesus quoted the first verse of Psalm 22 he had in his mind the whole psalm (something that is further suggested by the fact that mockery and the casting of lots for clothes both come from the same psalm). If this is the case then Jesus' words of despair have an additional tint.

This is because of the way in which the psalm ends.

Psalm 22.27–31   All the ends of the earth shall remember and turn to the Lord; and all the families of the nations shall worship before him. [28]For dominion belongs to the Lord, and he rules over the nations. [29]To him, indeed, shall all who sleep in the earth bow down; before him shall bow all who go down to the dust, and I shall live for him. [30]Posterity will serve him; future generations will be told about the Lord, [31]and proclaim his deliverance to a people yet unborn, saying that he has done it.

As with many psalms in the Old Testament that begin with lament, Psalm 22 ends with a statement of confidence in God. This statement of confidence includes the ends of the earth turning to God, and his deliverance being proclaimed to a people yet unborn.

If we add this to other features of Mark's Gospel that we can observe at this point in his narrative then the despair changes character somewhat. It is true that Jesus' cry from the cross is the lowest moment in the whole story. His enemies are apparently victorious, Jesus is alone abandoned apparently both by God and by his followers, and his death is fast approaching. No sooner does he die, however, than we realize that the darkness surrounding Jesus that is both real and figurative (15.33) is shot through with glimmers of light. First the curtain of the temple was torn in two and the centurion whose job it was to crucify Jesus declared him to be 'truly the Son of God' (on this more below). Then we discover that Jesus was not as alone as we thought he was, and the women who had followed and supported him through his life had not fled and were there near the cross until the end.

In other words we accompany Jesus down into the pit of despair but at the moment of utter desolation we begin to see that the darkness is not as thick as we believed it to be, and Jesus was not as abandoned as first appeared. This does not make his cry any less despairing or the desolation he felt any less real, but reminds us that human perception is not absolute and darkness never complete.

The curtain of the temple was torn in two

One of the themes that many people have noticed in Mark's Gospel is 'Messianic secrecy'. Time and time again Jesus, much to our surprise, tells people not to announce what he has done or who he is (see, for example, the man who was deaf in Mark 7.36). It is important, however, not to overplay the secrecy at the expense of revelation. There are three key moments of revelation in Mark's Gospel which reach their culmination at this point in his narrative. These three are Jesus' baptism, his transfiguration and his crucifixion. At each one of these points heaven breaks into earth and a voice speaks identifying Jesus as God's son.

- **Mark 1.10–11**   And just as he was coming up out of the water, he saw the heavens torn apart and the Spirit descending like a dove on him. [11]And a voice came from heaven, 'You are my Son, the Beloved; with you I am well pleased.'
- **Mark 9.7**   Then a cloud overshadowed them, and from the cloud there came a voice, 'This is my Son, the Beloved; listen to him!'
- **Mark 15.38–39**   And the curtain of the temple was torn in two, from top to bottom. [39]Now when the centurion, who stood facing him, saw that in this way he breathed his last, he said, 'Truly this man was God's Son!'

A few things are worth noticing. These three moments of revelation fall at, roughly, the beginning, middle and end of the Gospel. The first two moments of revelation involve God breaking through from heaven and identifying Jesus for who he is. At his moment of death, however, the revelation is significantly different.

The first difference is that it is not heaven but the curtain in the temple which is torn apart. This curtain was the curtain that separated the Holy of Holies from the rest of the temple. The Holy of Holies was the place where God descended to earth, and was widely viewed as the gateway to heaven. Tearing the temple curtain in two was an irreversible action – more so than the heavens being torn apart in Mark 1.10–11 – an action that now gave permanent access into the presence of God. Jesus' death was a moment of great revelation when heaven itself was revealed to earth.

The second difference is that this time when the voice spoke it was not God's voice speaking but someone else's. That someone else was someone from the ends of the earth (as Psalm 22.27 would put it), he was an absolute outsider, responsible in part for Jesus' death who nevertheless at the moment of dramatic revelation was the one who recognized and proclaimed who Jesus really was. Jesus' identity was a secret no more – even the centurion had worked out who he was.

The Son of God or a Son of God?

Sometimes people make the point that the centurion might have been saying something much less significant than we think he is (and certainly less significant than the point I've just made above).

The problem is that the Greek does not have a 'the' in front of Son or indeed in front of God (so it reads *huios theou*, literally son of God). The NRSV cleverly sidesteps the issue by translating it as 'God's Son' which avoids the need to say whether it is 'the son of God' or 'a son of God' (though intriguingly they put Son with an initial capital letter which implies they have a view!). While it is certainly true that *huios theou* could mean a son of God, the construction could equally mean 'a son of the God' or 'the son of the God'. This particular construction with the verb 'to be' does not need a 'the' for a 'the' to be implied.

In short we simply can't tell from the Greek whether the centurion meant to say 'a son of God' or 'the son of God'. My view is that the other two verses mentioned above (1.10–11 and 9.7) push us towards thinking that at least Mark – even if we do not know about the centurion – saw a huge significance in the centurion identifying Jesus as God's son.

In great contrast in Luke the centurion described Jesus not as God's son but as 'innocent'. The Greek word is *dikaios* and

---

> stands as a great contrast with Luke's words for the people Jesus was crucified alongside (*kakourgos* or evil-doers). It means much more than innocent, however, and could be equally translated as 'just' or 'righteous'.

In Matthew's Gospel it is not just the curtain in the temple that was torn in two but the very earth itself. The result of this tearing is that many saints were raised from the dead. For some people this episode causes all sorts of problems but it is important to recognize what Matthew expected us to understand from what happened.

> **Matthew 27.51–53** At that moment the curtain of the temple was torn in two, from top to bottom. The earth shook, and the rocks were split. [52]The tombs also were opened, and many bodies of the saints who had fallen asleep were raised. [53]After his resurrection they came out of the tombs and entered the holy city and appeared to many.

The crucial point is that Jesus' death meant that the created world itself was now completely different. Many, though not all, Jews of the first century believed that the dead would be raised at the end of this age and start of the next. Matthew's account therefore is making a significant statement: Jesus' death marked the start of the age to come. His willing sacrifice on the cross changed the world in which we live so dramatically that the age to come was inaugurated. This does not mean that it arrived in all its fullness. We are still to wait for the coming of the Son of Man on the clouds of glory, but the new age has begun. The kingdom has broken in, the world has now changed and we must live, as a result, in the light of that change.

Indeed it is possible that in Matthew's mind the tearing of the curtain in the temple was not just about giving us access to God but that it was a symbol of God himself breaking out of the temple. With Jesus' death he was no longer concealed behind a curtain in the temple but was at large in the world that he created, shaking its foundations and changing it forever.

Luke's Tearing of the Temple Curtain

Luke 23.44–45 It was now about noon, and darkness came over the whole land until three in the afternoon, [45]while the sun's light failed; and the curtain of the temple was torn in two.

In Luke's Gospel the tearing of the temple curtain is moved forward so that it coincides not with Jesus' death but with the darkness that falls over the whole land. As a result, it is downgraded to being a portent like the darkness rather than a marker of the changes wrought by Jesus' death. These changes, in my view, are marked instead by Jesus' conversation with the criminal on the cross (on which see more below).

Today you will be with me in Paradise

A very well-loved part of Luke's crucifixion narrative is Jesus' conversation with the 'evil-doer' on the cross.

Luke 23.40–43 But the other rebuked him, saying, 'Do you not fear God, since you are under the same sentence of condemnation? [41]And we indeed have been condemned justly, for we are getting what we deserve for our deeds, but this man has done nothing wrong.' [42]Then he said, 'Jesus, remember me when you come into your kingdom.' [43]He replied, 'Truly I tell you, today you will be with me in Paradise.'

It is loved for good reason. Here we see the overwhelming grace that flows from Jesus even at the point of his greatest agony. The criminal, unlike so many others surrounding Jesus at his crucifixion, acknowledged the genuineness of Jesus' kingdom and Jesus responded with the promise that this very day he would join Jesus in Paradise. The implication is that this evil-doer has, simply by responding and recognizing Jesus, been transferred from the category of evil-doer (*kakourgos*) to 'righteous' (*diakios*) like Jesus.

In my view, however, this is not all that is going on here. I would see this exchange as being the equivalent of Matthew's account of the dead rising. The word 'Paradise' comes from a Persian word for 'walled garden' but by this point in Jewish interpretation meant a very particular walled garden: the Garden of Eden. Tradition has it that after Adam and Eve were expelled the Garden was sealed up and would remain so until the age to come when it would be reopened and people would be able to eat of the fruit of the tree of life again. This is certainly a tradition reflected in Revelation 2.7.

> **Revelation 2.7**   Let anyone who has an ear listen to what the Spirit is saying to the churches. To everyone who conquers, I will give permission to eat from the tree of life that is in the paradise of God.

As a result Jesus is not just having a personal conversation with the now righteous, former evil-doer but is making a much bigger theological statement: today as a result of Jesus' death, Paradise, which was sealed until the end of the age, would be reopened and the now righteous man from the cross would join Jesus in the newly opened Paradise of God.

Behold your Son

A striking feature of John's account of the crucifixion are the differences between it and the other three Gospels. Many of the iconic features of the other accounts are simply missing in John. For example, the darkness over the land; the mockery of Jesus by those around the cross; the cry from Psalm 22.1; Jesus' final loud cry; the reaction of the centurion; and the tearing of the temple curtain.

John's Gospel, however, has another unique account: the dedication of Jesus' mother to the care of the beloved disciple.

> **John 19.25b-27** Meanwhile, standing near the cross of Jesus were his mother, and his mother's sister, Mary the wife of Clopas, and Mary Magdalene. When Jesus saw his mother and the disciple whom he loved standing beside her, he said to his mother, 'Woman, here is your son.' [27]Then he said to the disciple, 'Here is your mother.' And from that hour the disciple took her into his own home.

The first thing to notice is that John moves the women at the cross much more to centre stage. In Mark's Gospel we only discover that they were there after Jesus' death; in John's Gospel they are there throughout the last hours of Jesus' life. The question is, what is the significance of this action by Jesus?

One of the key points to recognize is that this account is close in many ways to the story of the Wedding at Cana right at the start of Jesus' ministry in John's Gospel. There, as here, Mary is addressed as 'woman'. There Jesus declared that his hour had not yet come; here his hour most certainly has come. There Mary's role in the events is questioned by Jesus; here her role as 'mother' as affirmed. The question Jesus asked of Mary in John 2.4 is notoriously difficult to translate. Literally the Greek reads 'Woman, what to me and to you?' The most obvious meaning of this is what connection is there between me and you? The answer to this question is provided here at the cross – she is his mother and he, her son. Jesus' passing of her into the care of another emphasizes this deep relationship of love.

In John's Gospel Jesus' death is, as we have expected all along, a moment of the revelation of his glory. It can often be hard in John to distinguish between Jesus' death, resurrection and ascension. This cross is where he is lifted up and his glory revealed to the world. It is the moment where his divinity comes triumphantly to the fore.

This vignette of human love then becomes vitally important. As so often in John's Gospel, Jesus' divinity is thoroughly laced with humanity. There can be no doubt that Jesus is fully God *and* fully human all the way through the Gospel. The care he shows for his mother reminds us of this here. Jesus has been lifted up, his glory has been revealed and at the same time we are reminded of his humanity, in the person of his human mother, for whom he cares. Once his hour has come, the question of John 2.4 can now be truly answered 'What to me and to you?' – you are my mother and I your son.

Jesus' death

The moment of Jesus' death in the four Gospels is slightly different in each Gospel. However they are not quite as far apart as the English translations appear to suggest – nor indeed are Matthew and Mark as close as the NRSV suggests.

- **Matthew 27.50** Then Jesus cried again with a loud voice and breathed his last.
- **Mark 15.37** Then Jesus gave a loud cry and breathed his last.
- **Luke 23.46** Then Jesus, crying with a loud voice, said, 'Father, into your hands I commend my spirit.' Having said this, he breathed his last.
- **John 19.30** When Jesus had received the wine, he said, 'It is finished.' Then he bowed his head and gave up his spirit.

Mark's version says literally that Jesus 'having let out a great sound breathed out'. This was a common euphemism for 'died'. The verb 'breathed out' (*exepneusen* in Greek) is a verb connected to the noun *pneuma* (breath or spirit). Matthew's version is close but different, literally: Jesus 'having cried out with a great sound, let his breath (or spirit) go'. The noun used here is *pneuma* so could mean either breath or spirit or both.

This close connection is emphasized by Luke which has the word *pneuma* again for 'Father into your hands I entrust my spirit' (or breath?) and then picks up the more Markan version 'having said these things he breathed out' (*exepneusen*). John has 'and he bowed his head and handed over his spirit or breath' (*pneuma*). As a result the same root is used in all Gospels, it is just that sometimes it is translated 'breath' and sometimes 'spirit'. The breath/spirit overlap is very strong here and while *we* might understand it solely as stopping breathing, in the Ancient world this was also seen as giving up one's spirit.

I commend my spirit

It is no coincidence that Luke's Gospel is the one which places the greatest focus on the surrendering of the spirit. Here Jesus hands the spirit back to his Father in preparation for that spirit to be returned to Jesus' followers at Pentecost. In Luke this is no petering out of breath but a deliberate handing over of Jesus' spirit, to be kept until a later time.

---

* * *

Reflection

Atonement theory focuses our attention strongly on the question of what Jesus' death has done for us and how it was achieved. This is very important, and explorations of the nature of Jesus' atoning death stand appropriately at the centre of our Christian faith and practice. However, it is important not to focus on them so entirely that we miss another strand which was vitally important for the Gospel writers: Jesus' death was not just about us as individuals, it also had a cosmic impact.

The world itself was changed by Jesus' death, from the more minor element of the sky being dark as he hung on the cross, to the much more major tearing open of the temple curtain, the wrenching open of the graves and the consequent opening of Paradise. Matthew and Luke in particular are clear that Jesus' death ushered in a new age – the age to come – we still await it in all its fullness but it has begun. God's kingdom has broken into our world and heaven is no longer veiled from earth by the curtain in the temple. With Jesus' death the world changed for good and part of the task of Jesus' disciples is to find a way to live now in acknowledgement that the new age has already begun.

It is Paul who talks much more about the practicalities of this than the Gospels do, but it is why he puts so much stress on the character of Christian living. This is not just an arbitrary list of 'oughts' but an attempt to shape what it might look like to live as citizens of God's kingdom, as members of the new age inaugurated by Jesus' death and resurrection.

The Burial of Jesus

Matthew 27.57–66; Mark 15.42–47; Luke 23.50–56;
John 19.31–42

Ensuring Jesus was dead

> **John 19.31-37** Since it was the day of Preparation, the Jews did not want the bodies left on the cross during the sabbath, especially because that sabbath was a day of great solemnity. So they asked Pilate to have the legs of the crucified men broken and the bodies removed. [32]Then the soldiers came and broke the legs of the first and of the other who had been crucified with him. [33]But when they came to Jesus and saw that he was already dead, they did not break his legs. [34]Instead, one of the soldiers pierced his side with a spear, and at once blood and water came out. [35](He who saw this has testified so that you also may believe. His testimony is true, and he knows that he tells the truth.) [36]These things occurred so that the scripture might be fulfilled, 'None of his bones shall be broken.' [37]And again another passage of scripture says, 'They will look on the one whom they have pierced.'

John's Gospel is the only narrative which recounts the need to ensure that Jesus was really dead and to speed it up lest he still be alive once the festival began (this of course would be superfluous in any other Gospel since in them the festival had already begun). It does provide a helpful explanation, however, which is not provided in Matthew, Mark or Luke, for why Jesus' body was not left to hang on the cross indefinitely as a warning to those who passed by as was Roman custom. Indeed it coheres with a suggestion by Philo (*In Flaccum* 10.83–84) that on the eve of a feast bodies were sometimes taken down and given to relatives to bury.

It might appear that John's intention is to provide an assurance (which he backs up with a declaration of eyewitness veracity) that Jesus was in fact dead. The problem is that to our modern,

Western eyes it raises so many problems that much ink has been spilled on the attempt to understand it. The nub of the matter is that a dead body cannot bleed as the heart has stopped pumping, so blood (and water) flowing from Jesus' side suggests that he wasn't actually dead and thus proves the opposite of what John appears to intend.

The centurion

An interesting possible connection between Mark and John's account at this point is that the centurion overseeing Jesus' death is summoned in Mark by Pilate to offer assurance that he had in fact died. Since the presence of two centurions is unlikely, this centurion was probably the one who declared Jesus to be God's son. If that is the case then if we connect Mark and John, that centurion could well have been the one who pierced Jesus' side with a spear.

It is possible, however, that John's intention was theological not historical. This is certainly suggested by the parenthesis in verse 35 which states that it is included 'so that you also may believe'. It is interesting to note that water and blood is also referred to in 1 John 5.7–8: 'There are three that testify: the Spirit and the water and the blood, and these three agree.' What is harder to fathom is what this might mean. One possibility is that spirit, water and blood are integrally linked in Johannine spirituality and so needed to be present here at the moment that Jesus gave up his spirit.

This brings us no closer, however, to what it means. Some tie the event into the flowing of living water in John 7.38–39; some to Eucharistic allusions; some link it to sacrifice and the need at a sacrifice for blood to flow freely. In reality, while it is likely that this event did have some level of theological significance it is hard to pin down exactly what it was.

Burying Jesus

> **Mark 15.42–47** When evening had come, and since it was the day of Preparation, that is, the day before the sabbath, [43]Joseph of Arimathea, a respected member of the council, who was also himself waiting expectantly for the kingdom of God, went boldly to Pilate and asked for the body of Jesus. [44]Then Pilate wondered if he were already dead; and summoning the centurion, he asked him whether he had been dead for some time. [45]When he learned from the centurion that he was dead, he granted the body to Joseph. [46]Then Joseph bought a linen cloth, and taking down the body, wrapped it in the linen cloth, and laid it in a tomb that had been hewn out of the rock. He then rolled a stone against the door of the tomb. [47]Mary Magdalene and Mary the mother of Joses saw where the body was laid.

Joseph of Arimathea is said to have been a member of the Sanhedrin (and in John's Gospel is joined by Nicodemus who was also part of the Sanhedrin). This is important not only because he would have had the authority to approach Pilate to ask for Jesus' body but also because it reveals for the first time in the account that the Sanhedrin was not unanimous in its opposition to Jesus.

The description of the tomb here, and later when the women return with the spices, reveals that it was a substantial family tomb such as would have been common for wealthier members of society. These tombs were often quite elaborate and had a number of shelves and tunnels off the main entrance to enable a large number of people to be buried in a single tomb (some could contain 60 bodies). The whole complex was sealed with a stone rolled over the entrance.

John's Gospel clears up any potential confusion over multiple bodies by stating that it was a new tomb in which no one had ever been laid, lest anyone might think that the women thought that Jesus had risen from the dead when really they were looking at the wrong shelf!

* * *

Reflection

One of the features of Jesus' death that is easy to miss, because it is only ever implicit in the texts, is that his death completely redefined what makes for a good death. In Jewish tradition three key features defined a good death: living to a good old age (like the righteous in the Old Testament); leaving a son behind to maintain your line (note the importance of this in 1 and 2 Kings where stress is always placed on sons ruling in their father's stead), and being buried in your ancestral tomb along with your forebears.

Against this tradition, Jesus had a spectacularly bad death: he died young; left no children and was buried in a borrowed tomb. Jesus' death was, of course, not a bad death at all and blows apart our expectation of what dying well means. Today we might define a good death in different terms: without undue pain; with our loved ones beside us and with time to say our farewells.

But Jesus' death speaks a challenge as much now as it did then. Our definitions of a good death are invariably about us and what we might wish to attain. Jesus' definition of a good death was about others and what he might give them. Above all Jesus' idea of a good death was about a love so great, so infinite and immeasurable that he was prepared to die to ensure that it was expressed to the full.

On Darkness and Light

(Based on reflections drawn from comments above on Mark's crucifixion narrative.)

In our own moments of deep darkness,
   when despair takes its grip on our souls
   when we feel abandoned and alone
   when the presence of God is at best a dim memory
   and we echo deep within us Jesus' cry of desolation
   'My God, my God why have you forsaken me?'
   then, at the bottom of the pit, when we can sink no more,
May our grip tighten around the knowledge
   that Psalm 22 does not end at verse one
   that Jesus was not alone and the women had never left
   that light was flickering and hope was stirring
   that the world was about to change forever.

In our own moments of deep darkness
   when despair takes its grip on our souls,
May we have the strength to hold on to the assurance
   that beyond darkness there is light
   beyond despair there is hope
   beyond dying there is living
   beyond forsakenness there is, always, the love of God.

In our own moments of deep darkness
   may this hope carry us through
   the days, months, and sometimes years
   until the new dawn's first rays of light
   touch our souls with the warmth of an Easter morning.

5

The Empty Tomb and
Resurrection Appearances

The part of the story of Jesus which is, possibly, the most dissimi-
lar in the Gospels is the resurrection accounts. No two Gospels
have exactly the same stories or way of telling what happened.
This could be read sceptically as an indication that each Gospel
writer was simply making it up, or it can be read as a sign of the
overwhelming importance of the events. Each Gospel writer had
a favourite tale to tell that, for them, communicated the wonder
of what happened and so simply felt unable to miss their own
favourite account out. If we bring Paul in at this point, he states
that Jesus appeared to over 500 people after his resurrection (1
Corinthians 15.6), indicating perhaps that the Gospel writers are
only scratching the surface of the stories that could have been told
about his resurrection appearances.

The accounts about what happened on Easter morning and
beyond fall into three main types:

- An encounter at the empty tomb with angels.
- A meeting with Jesus near the tomb as assurance that he did
  really rise from the dead.
- An experience of the risen Christ away from the tomb often
  with a commissioning to further action.

By and large, with a few exceptions which we will explore as we
come across them, the encounters at the tomb are demonstrations
that Jesus was risen and those away from the tomb commission
the disciples to action and proclamation as we will see below.

At the tomb

All the Gospels have some kind of encounter at the tomb but this is where the more important question of dissimilarity occurs. It is easy to explain the contrasting accounts as simply separate traditions about Jesus' resurrection, but when the same account is told differently this gets more complicated. What is interesting, however, is that while there are differences they are all set around a theme.

For example each of the Gospels has its own list of women who went to the tomb – but they are all women:

- **Mark:** Mary Magdalene, Mary the mother of James, and Salome.
- **Matthew:** Mary Magdalene and the other Mary.
- **Luke:** The women who had come with him from Galilee.
- **John:** Mary Magdalene.

In the same way each Gospel tells a slightly different version of what happened at the tomb but they all include a reference to the stone rolled away and a vision of angels:

- **Mark:** The women found the stone rolled away, the tomb empty, had a message from an angel and ran away.
- **Matthew:** There was an earthquake, an angel descended and rolled the stone away; the guards were rendered unconscious; the women received a message – which they passed on.
- **Luke:** The women found the stone rolled away, the tomb empty and saw two angels; they received no message for the disciples but they passed on that he had risen and were not believed (though Peter went to see the tomb for himself).
- **John:** Mary saw that the stone had been removed; got Peter and the beloved disciple who both saw the empty tomb; Mary saw two angels and then encountered Jesus in the garden and received the message that Jesus was ascending to his Father.

What this indicates is that the underlying commonalities are strong but they became told differently among separate groups of people.

He is Not Here

Mark 16.1–8

> **Mark 16.1–8** When the sabbath was over, Mary Magdalene, and Mary the mother of James, and Salome bought spices, so that they might go and anoint him. [2]And very early on the first day of the week, when the sun had risen, they went to the tomb. [3]They had been saying to one another, 'Who will roll away the stone for us from the entrance to the tomb?' [4]When they looked up, they saw that the stone, which was very large, had already been rolled back. [5]As they entered the tomb, they saw a young man, dressed in a white robe, sitting on the right side; and they were alarmed. [6]But he said to them, 'Do not be alarmed; you are looking for Jesus of Nazareth, who was crucified. He has been raised; he is not here. Look, there is the place they laid him. [7]But go, tell his disciples and Peter that he is going ahead of you to Galilee; there you will see him, just as he told you.' [8]So they went out and fled from the tomb, for terror and amazement had seized them; and they said nothing to anyone, for they were afraid.

The account that stands out from all the others is Mark's since it, alone, has no resurrection appearance. All we have in Mark is an empty tomb and an angelic message that Jesus would go before the women to Galilee. The end of the whole Gospel is abrupt; 'they said nothing to anyone, for they were afraid', and so bewildering that Christian tradition assumed the original ending had been lost and provided others. There are two key ones, a longer and a shorter ending, but they are so different from the rest of the Gospel in style that few scholars are convinced that they are original to the Gospel. Many scholars today would simply accept that the abrupt ending was the original one.

Indeed it might be the clumsiness of the ending that is the point in Mark. It is apparently even clumsier in Greek than in English. In Greek it reads literally 'They were afraid for.' The last sentence is simply two words ('they were afraid' and 'for'), but, as any Greek scholar will tell you, in a two-word sentence where you have the word 'for' it must go last because 'for' must always be the second word in a sentence. The whole effect, though, is of a cliffhanger, will the women go and tell or not?

A white robe

Although the description of the angels differs slightly in each Gospel (Matthew and Mark have one angel and Luke and John have two), the feature that joins them all is their appearance. In Mark and John they wear white; in Matthew the angel's appearance was like lightning and his clothes white; in Luke the angels were dazzling. The significance of this is that it is a sign that the angels have come directly from God. The descriptions of God in heaven all associate him with white clothing and bright light and the description of the angels as similarly clad is designed to remove all doubt whether these are 'just' people or angels from God.

This is where our attention must turn to the message they are given by the angels: 'Go, tell his disciples.' For the first time in Mark's Gospel the command has changed. It is no longer 'Tell no one', now it is 'Go, tell'. The secrecy is over, the revelation is complete. Now is the time to go and proclaim everything that they know. The command at the tomb is vitally important, Jesus' identity is a secret no more – the time has come to shout it from the rooftops.

But the women fled just as the men had done. The women, unlike the male disciples, did not flee at the crucifixion; they stayed and they sought to serve Jesus in his death just as they had during his lifetime. But when the moment came to 'Go, tell' even their staying power crumbled and they fled. The Gospel of Mark is a story of failed discipleship from beginning to end. Time and time again the disciples misunderstand Jesus and then ultimately they let him down and run away. Even the women who remained faithful for longer flee. As the Gospel screeches to an undignified halt in 16.8, all we can hear is feet running in the opposite direction.

The irony, however, is that we know that this is not how it ended. If the women had really said nothing to anyone then we wouldn't know that they had run off at the end of the Gospel. We, the readers, know that eventually they did 'Go, tell' as they were commanded and that slowly with the male disciples they did return and did begin the task of proclamation. The ungainly ending of the Gospel offers us both a challenge and forgiveness.

The challenge is whether we will respond any better than the male disciples who ran off at the first hurdle; or the female disciples who ran off at the second. This should not make us feel in any way superior. The disciples were well advised to run away. In Mark's Gospel it is very clear that the way of discipleship is the way of the cross. If we follow in Jesus' footsteps we will discover what it means to pick up our cross and follow him. It may be that running off in hot pursuit of the earliest disciples is the more sensible course of action. This is where the forgiveness comes in. The disciples ran away, but we know from the fact that we are now reading the Gospel that they came back. We may fail just as they did but when we do we can be assured that we are in good company, as we seek to return and find the words to 'Go, tell' everything that we know about Jesus, Son of God, Messiah.

* * *

Reflection

Mark's Gospel ends as it began – abruptly. Just as Jesus erupts into the pages of our Gospel in Mark 1.1, so the female disciples leave them just as suddenly in 16.8. In many ways the ending is unsatisfactory. It simply stops, but it does so for a reason – because it is not the end. Mark, more than any of the other

Gospels, has his eye on us his readers all the way through. In Mark's Gospel there are three key groups of characters: the Jewish leaders, the crowd and the disciples. As we come to the end of the Gospel we realize that there has been one more group all the way through the Gospel: those of us who are reading it. We, the readers, make a fourth unseen group and Mark is speaking to us throughout the Gospel. The question that he asks is, will we respond like the Jewish leaders, like the crowd, like the disciples or somehow differently? Will we be able to break out of our expectations, our set ideas and our distractions for long enough to recognize who Jesus really was and is and to respond to him?

Mark 16.8, with its unsatisfactory ending, issues the clearest invitation to us the readers to stop now being readers and to start being participants in the narrative. It invites us to pick up the story and to live out its ending in our own lives. The women were challenged to 'Go, tell' and ran away. Today, we too are being challenged to 'Go, tell'. The question is whether we too will run away for good, whether we will run away and return later, or even whether we might respond immediately (one of Mark's favourite words) and run to share the good news of Jesus Christ, Son of God, Saviour.

The Empty Tomb in the Other Gospels

Matthew 28.1–15; Luke 24.1–11; John 20.1–2

Having looked at Mark's account of the empty tomb, it is worth turning our attention briefly to the empty tomb accounts in the other Gospels.

Matthew 28.1–15 After the Sabbath, as the first day of the week was dawning, Mary Magdalene and the other Mary went to see the tomb. [2]And suddenly there was a great earthquake; for an angel of the Lord, descending from heaven, came and rolled back the stone and sat on it. [3]His appearance was like lightning, and his clothing white as snow. [4]For fear of him the guards shook and became like dead men. [5]But the angel said to the women, 'Do not be afraid; I know that you are looking for Jesus who was crucified. [6]He is not here; for he has been raised, as he said. Come, see the place where he lay. [7]Then go quickly and tell his disciples, "He has been raised from the dead, and indeed he is going ahead of you to Galilee; there you will see him." This is my message for you.' [8]So they left the tomb quickly with fear and great joy, and ran to tell his disciples.

[9]Suddenly Jesus met them and said, 'Greetings!' And they came to him, took hold of his feet, and worshiped him. [10]Then Jesus said to them, 'Do not be afraid; go and tell my brothers to go to Galilee; there they will see me.'

[11]While they were going, some of the guard went into the city and told the chief priests everything that had happened. [12]After the priests had assembled with the elders, they devised a plan to give a large sum of money to the soldiers, [13]telling them, 'You must say, "His disciples came by night and stole him away while we were asleep." [14]If this comes to the governor's ears, we will satisfy him and keep you out of trouble.' [15]So they took the money and did as they were directed. And this story is still told among the Jews to this day.

One of the crucial differences between Matthew's Gospel and the other Gospels is that in Matthew the story does continue and the women did go and tell the disciples that Jesus was raised from the dead. There are some other features as well, however, that are worth noting. The first is that the women are not the only primary characters in Matthew's scene – the guards are important too. Matthew is the only Gospel that mentions a guard on the tomb. This account more than any other in the resurrection appearances seems to be responding to a later tradition.

Matthew is clearly aware of a rumour that Jesus was not really risen from the dead and so this account allows him to counter that rumour with a narrative from the resurrection itself. The presence of the guards at the tomb makes it very clear that in Matthew's view this is a lie, since they know and saw, just as the women did, the angel rolling the stone from the tomb. If they were both present as the stone was rolled away it simply was not possible for the body to have been removed earlier.

The angel and the stone

One of the intriguing features of Matthew's Gospel is that the rolling away of the stone gains a different significance. In all of the other Gospels the stone is rolled away before the women arrive at the tomb. We are left to assume therefore that it is rolled away so that the risen Jesus could get out. In Matthew, however, it is rolled away while the women and the guards are there, in front of them. The angels tell the women that 'He is not here' and so indicate that he is already risen. The rolling away of the stone therefore is not to aid Jesus' exit, but to prove his resurrection.

One of the key differences between the resurrection accounts is when the risen Jesus was first seen. John famously has an encounter between Mary and Jesus at the tomb itself; Matthew on the way back from the tomb; Luke a good way from Jerusalem on the road to Emmaus and Mark not at all. The key feature of the

JOURNEY TO THE EMPTY TOMB

appearance in Matthew is the assurance of the truth of Jesus' resurrection.

A nice possible twist in Matthew's account is that on seeing the risen Jesus the women (as the disciples do subsequently in Galilee) worshipped Jesus. The text indicates that this worship took the form of full prostration before Jesus, since they took hold of his feet. It is possible that this detail has significance. Some beliefs about ghosts in the Ancient world stated that ghosts have no feet. The fact that the women were able to worship him by taking hold of his feet may be another of Matthew's motifs, to counter scepticism. His body was not stolen as the guards knew full well and he was not a ghost since the women took hold of his feet; the only other conclusion to draw, therefore, was that Jesus truly was risen from the dead.

Looking in the Tomb

Luke 24.12; John 20.3–10

> **John 20.3–10** Then Peter and the other disciple set out and went toward the tomb. [4]The two were running together, but the other disciple outran Peter and reached the tomb first. [5]He bent down to look in and saw the linen wrappings lying there, but he did not go in. [6]Then Simon Peter came, following him, and went into the tomb. He saw the linen wrappings lying there, [7]and the cloth that had been on Jesus' head, not lying with the linen wrappings but rolled up in a place by itself. [8]Then the other disciple, who reached the tomb first, also went in, and he saw and believed; [9]for as yet they did not understand the scripture, that he must rise from the dead. [10]Then the disciples returned to their homes.

If Matthew's response to scepticism about Jesus' resurrection is to counter the rumour that his body was stolen and that he was a ghost, Luke and John refute the suggestion that his body might still be in there. This is where John's additional detail that this was a new tomb becomes vitally important. In a large tomb, it is possible that there could have been dozens of dead bodies inside. If it were new and there were no other bodies in there then the lack of Jesus' body becomes proof of his resurrection. Both Luke and John have Peter (or Peter and the beloved disciple) coming to see that the tomb was in fact completely empty of all bodies.

But there is another strand that comes to the fore here too (and one that we will pick up again when we look at the Emmaus road story): it is one thing to see the empty tomb, it is quite another to believe that Jesus was risen from the dead. With the exception of Mark, all the Gospels tell the narrative of the movement from recognition that the tomb was empty to a belief that Jesus was risen in a different way. In Matthew it is short and sweet. The women meet Jesus, worship him and go and tell the disciples (though as we will see even then there is an element of doubt in their mind). In Luke the key moment of realization happens on the road to Emmaus and then again when he met with them in Jerusalem. In John the realization takes various stages: the beloved disciple believed just by seeing the empty tomb; Mary believed by meeting Jesus; the other disciples by seeing the risen Jesus, and Thomas, at last, by putting his hands in Jesus' scars. This movement from observation to belief in John is told beat by beat in acknowledgement that it is, for all of us, a journey which may take some time.

Resurrection Appearances 1: Assurance that He is Risen

Sensing the risen Jesus

John 20.11–18, 20.24–29

John 20.11-18   But Mary stood weeping outside the tomb. As she wept, she bent over to look into the tomb; [12]and she saw two angels in white, sitting where the body of Jesus had been lying, one at the head and the other at the feet. [13]They said to her, 'Woman, why are you weeping?' She said to them, 'They have taken away my Lord, and I do not know where they have laid him.' [14]When she had said this, she turned around and saw Jesus standing there, but she did not know that it was Jesus.

[15]Jesus said to her, 'Woman, why are you weeping? Whom are you looking for?' Supposing him to be the gardener, she said to him, 'Sir, if you have carried him away, tell me where you have laid him, and I will take him away.' [16]Jesus said to her, 'Mary!' She turned and said to him in Hebrew, 'Rabbouni!' (which means Teacher). [17]Jesus said to her, 'Do not hold on to me, because I have not yet ascended to the Father. But go to my brothers and say to them, "I am ascending to my Father and your Father, to my God and your God."' [18]Mary Magdalene went and announced to the disciples, 'I have seen the Lord'; and she told them that he had said these things to her.

John 20.24-29   But Thomas (who was called the Twin), one of the twelve, was not with them when Jesus came. [25]So the other disciples told him, 'We have seen the Lord.' But he said to them, 'Unless I see the mark of the nails in his hands, and put my finger in the mark of the nails and my hand in his side, I will not believe.' [26]A week later his disciples were again in the house, and Thomas was with them. Although the doors were shut, Jesus came and stood among them and said, 'Peace be with you.' [27]Then he said to Thomas, 'Put your finger here and see my hands. Reach out your hand and put it in my side. Do not doubt but believe.'

> [28]Thomas answered him, 'My Lord and my God!' [29]Jesus said to him, 'Have you believed because you have seen me? Blessed are those who have not seen and yet have come to believe.'

One of the best-loved stories of Jesus' resurrection is the story of Mary's encounter with the risen Jesus at the tomb itself. We often split this story – that of Mary recognizing Jesus – from one of the other key Johannine resurrection events – that of Thomas seeing and believing, but if we do we miss one of the key strands of John's narrative here. What is very important in this part of John is that John is playing with the theme of sense and believing. Here Mary 'saw' but did not believe because she didn't recognize Jesus. It was only when she heard Jesus' voice that she believed. In the Thomas story Thomas 'heard' what the other disciples said but did not believe because he had not seen and touched (interestingly we are not told whether seeing would have been enough by itself). Both Mary and Thomas needed additional sensory help (hearing the voice of Jesus and touching his wounds) for them to be able to recognize and believe.

What this strand reminds us is that even John, whose statements are so clear and confident about who Jesus was and who draws light and shade so starkly, recognized quite how hard a task it was to see the risen Christ and then to believe. Both Mary and Thomas needed to use their own senses of hearing and touch to help them understand and hence believe. This raises the crucially important question of whether this is still true today. Christian worship can be a multisensory experience but often it is not. The experience of both Mary and Thomas raises the question of whether we need to be much more intentional about the senses and how they can help people to move from incomprehension and lack of recognition to belief.

Why did they not recognize Jesus?

Mary is not the only person in the resurrection accounts to fail to recognize Jesus. It is also a key feature of the road to Emmaus. This raises the question of what Jesus' resurrection body was like and why his disciples, who knew him so well, failed to identify him. It is possible that the answer is the most prosaic one: because they simply didn't expect to see him, so when they did, they did not recognize him. It is also possible that they didn't recognize him because he looked different.

If this is the case it tells us something important about our own resurrection bodies which Paul in 1 Corinthians 15 is very keen to link with Jesus' resurrection body. If Jesus' resurrection body looked different, then ours may too. Having said that however, there is an important point of continuity between Jesus' pre- and post-resurrection body: his crucifixion scars. This suggests that though our bodies are transformed at resurrection, the very things we might wish to lose – the scars we received in the course of living – are the very things that remain.

One of the many reasons why people love the story of Mary's encounter with Jesus is that it provides a beautifully worked illustration of John 10.3 and 27: 'The gatekeeper opens the gate for him, and the sheep hear his voice. He calls his own sheep by name and leads them out', and 'My sheep hear my voice. I know them, and they follow me.' She is not persuaded by Jesus of the facts of his resurrection, he does not argue her into comprehension – he simply called her name and because she belonged to him she heard that calling deep within her and responded. It is, for me, the perfect illustration of faith. Apologetics is very important. The need to argue the philosophical basis of our faith has never been greater, but the problem is that the very best arguments about faith are not why I believe – nor have I met many people for whom this would be true either. The reason why I believe and continue to do so is the gentle calling of my name – that calling to the deep essence of who I really am – which time and time again draws me back into recognition and worship of the shepherd who calls.

We noted above the importance of 'sense' in bringing both Mary and Thomas to a moment of recognition of who Jesus really was. We cannot leave this passage, therefore, without reflecting briefly on Jesus' command to Mary not to 'hold on to me, because I have not yet ascended to the Father' (John 20.17). This seems to be contradictory. Why is Mary not to touch, whereas Thomas is? The apparent contradiction is enhanced by the Latin translation of the text which, unusually, is well known since it is used as a title of a number of iconic paintings of the scene: '*noli me tangere*' means 'do not touch'. So it seems to set up a direct conflict between the Mary account and the Thomas one.

In reality no such conflict exists. Thomas is invited by Jesus to 'probe' his wounds in order to convince him that this was really Jesus; in contrast Mary is instructed not to cling to Jesus. This alternative translation makes what is going on much clearer. Mary is not to cling to Jesus because he has yet ascended. The implication of this is that having heard his promise to be with his disciples permanently, Mary understood it to mean that his resurrection body was how he would be with them permanently. This was not the case – Jesus would be with them through his Spirit – not his resurrection body. If Mary were to cling to him she would only end up being bereaved all over again.

The Road to Emmaus

Luke 24.13–35

Luke 24.13-35 Now on that same day two of them were going to a village called Emmaus, about seven miles from Jerusalem, [14]and talking with each other about all these things that had happened. [15]While they were talking and discussing, Jesus himself came near and went with them, [16]but their eyes were kept from recognizing him. [17]And he said to them, 'What are you discussing with each other while you walk along?' They stood still, looking sad.

[18]Then one of them, whose name was Cleopas, answered him, 'Are you the only stranger in Jerusalem who does not know the things that have taken place there in these days?' [19]He asked them, 'What things?' They replied, 'The things about Jesus of Nazareth, who was a prophet mighty in deed and word before God and all the people, [20]and how our chief priests and leaders handed him over to be condemned to death and crucified him. [21]But we had hoped that he was the one to redeem Israel. Yes, and besides all this, it is now the third day since these things took place. [22]Moreover, some women of our group astounded us. They were at the tomb early this morning [23]and when they did not find his body there, they came back and told us that they had indeed seen a vision of angels who said that he was alive. [24]Some of those who were with us went to the tomb and found it just as the women had said; but they did not see him.'

[25]Then he said to them, 'Oh, how foolish you are, and how slow of heart to believe all that the prophets have declared! [26]Was it not necessary that the Messiah should suffer these things and then enter into his glory?' [27]Then beginning with Moses and all the prophets, he interpreted to them the things about himself in all the scriptures.

[28]As they came near the village to which they were going, he walked ahead as if he were going on. [29]But they urged him strongly, saying, 'Stay with us, because it is almost evening and the day is now nearly over.' So he went in to stay with them. [30]When he was at the table with them, he took bread, blessed and broke it, and gave it to them. [31]Then their eyes were opened, and they recognized him; and he vanished from their sight. [32]They said to each other, 'Were not our hearts burning within us while he was talking to us on the road, while he was opening the scriptures to us?'

[33]That same hour they got up and returned to Jerusalem; and they found the eleven and their companions gathered together.

> [34]They were saying, 'The Lord has risen indeed, and he has appeared to Simon!' [35]Then they told what had happened on the road, and how he had been made known to them in the breaking of the bread.

It is hard to know whether to put the story of the encounter with Jesus on the road to Emmaus in the category of post-empty tomb 'assurance of resurrection' stories or in the later away-from-the-tomb commissioning stories. The challenge is that this is most definitely away from the tomb but Luke does not have any other 'assurance of resurrection' stories so it fulfils that role in Luke. As a result, in my mind, it falls into a similar category as the Mary story that we looked at above. Indeed it is very similar in some ways. In both neither Mary nor the two disciples recognize Jesus but then the moment of recognition occurs, and they are transformed. As a result, although away from the tomb, this story fits much better with the other empty tomb appearances than with the later accounts.

Where was Emmaus?

The location is not easy to tie down. Even the distance from Jerusalem is unclear. Some manuscripts have 'sixty stades' (the Roman measurement of a stade is about 607 feet or 1.85 metres). This makes the distance around 7 miles or 11 kilometres, but other manuscripts have 'one hundred and sixty stades' or 18 miles/29 kilometres.

There are nine different possible locations for Emmaus and that fact should caution us against attempting to tie down its location too carefully. Its key feature is that it was a long walk and the disciples arrived exhausted but, despite that, were able to run back to Jerusalem with the good news of the risen Jesus.

One of the oddest features of Luke's account is that the disciples are leaving Jerusalem. As they tell Jesus when they meet him, they have heard that Jesus was risen from the dead, the women have told them about the empty tomb, and others have been to see it too. Why, then, are they leaving Jerusalem and why are they so downcast? Indeed the word 'sad', used to describe their demeanour in verse 17, would be better translated as 'downcast'. They are devastated and look it.

Luke compounds this with their account to Jesus of how they had hoped that Jesus was going to be the one to redeem Israel. Here we meet Lukan irony again. Just as on the cross Jesus revealed that he was the saviour of the world precisely by not saving himself, so here he has redeemed Israel – he has died and risen again. What more could they want? What this tells us, however, is that they did not understand the significance of what had happened. The resurrection was something of a mystery and they were leaving Jerusalem disappointed and sick at heart that their hopes had not been realized. Contrary to what they thought, there was nothing more that needed to happen in the world. Instead they needed to travel to a place in themselves from which they could recognize what had already happened.

One of the intriguing features of the account, however, is that the two disciples do not seem to have been in entire agreement with each other. The NRSV downgrades the language Luke uses here. When Jesus first met these disciples they were in the middle of a 'discussion' according to the NRSV. In verse 14 they are said to be talking, in 15 talking and discussing, and then Jesus asked them what they were discussing in verse 17. The Greek suggests something altogether less polite. The first word used in verse 14 is *homileo*, converse. This is repeated in verse 15 but then added to the word *suzēteō* which is better translated as dispute than discuss. By the time Jesus asked them what they were doing in verse 17 he asked them literally 'what are these words that you are throwing against each other?' This strikes me as much more of an argument than a 'discussion'.

Who were the two disciples?

This leads us on to the question of the identity of these two disciples. Who they were can be no more than a point of speculation, but it is interesting to note that one of them was named: Cleopas. The name Cleopas was short for Cleopatros and could well have been the equivalent of Clopas, a name mentioned in John's Gospel. There in John we meet not Clopas but his wife Mary at the crucifixion. It is impossible to know for sure, but it is not beyond the bounds of possibility that the two disciples on the road to Emmaus are married to each other and that Jesus intervened in a marital dispute.

The crucial question for this passage is, if in John's Gospel it was hearing Jesus say her name that helped Mary to recognize who Jesus was, what was it in this account that brought about recognition? The conundrum is that, although Jesus spent the journey unpacking scripture for the disciples, this does not appear to have been the factor that caused them to recognize him. They looked back to it in retrospect but didn't appear to recognize it at the time.

Christian tradition has focused much more on the breaking of the bread as an action so characteristic of Jesus that it revealed his identity to the two disciples. This is certainly suggested by Luke since the disciples when recounting what had happened report that he 'had been made known to them in the breaking of the bread' (Luke 24.35). The question is how. The problem is that the blessing and breaking of bread was something that would have been done at the start of every Jewish meal and so would have been a normal activity at the start of the meal. Nevertheless there was clearly something that marked out this blessing and breaking from any other normal blessing and breaking. It could have been that Jesus had a strikingly characteristic way of breaking bread; or it could have been that in lifting up his hands to break the bread the scars in them were revealed (to borrow an image from John's Gospel). Another possibility is that it was the fact that he broke bread at all. The person who normally blessed and broke the bread was the host of the meal. Jesus, who was thought to be unknown to the two disciples, assumed the role of host. Could that have been the factor that caused them to recognize him?

It could have been all or none of these that caused recognition to dawn. The reality is that while the breaking of the bread was the 'moment' in which recognition took place, the disciples had been on an inner journey to match their outer one from Jerusalem to Emmaus. In the company of Jesus they travelled from disillusionment to inspiration; from incomprehension to understanding; from despair to hope. The company of Jesus, the opportunity to express their disappointment, the unpacking of the scriptures and one other factor all brought them to the moment where they could recognize Jesus in the breaking of the bread. The one other factor is, in my view, the fact that they invited him into their house. At the start of the narrative they were so self-absorbed with their grief and the fight they were having that they could not look beyond themselves. At the end, they looked outwards to the needs of this stranger that they had met. I wonder whether it was the simple looking outwards that tipped the balance into recognition moments later.

* * *

Reflection

As we have already noted, the Gospel narratives (with the exception of Mark) all tell the story of a journey towards the recognition of the risen Christ, but none more so than Luke. As a biblical scholar, I have often wished that the disciples could have written down what Jesus said as he unpacked the scriptures for them. How wonderful it would be to have what Jesus himself said about the Bible and its meaning but, on reflection, I wonder if that is to miss the point entirely. What Jesus saw in the two miserable, angry disciples was the need to journey beyond themselves. This journey from their own self-absorption to a recognition of Jesus involved the body (walking to Emmaus), the mind (the conversation about the scriptures) and the spirit (inviting Jesus in to eat with them). It was only once these three combined that Jesus became known in the breaking of the bread.

It is easy to assume that our spiritual journeys need only to be monofaceted: that it is about our spirits and nothing else. The road to Emmaus points us in a very different direction. In order to encounter the risen Jesus and to recognize him for who he really is, we need to journey with body, mind and spirit. We need to move physically, we need to move intellectually and we need to move spiritually and emotionally. Most of all we need to move beyond ourselves, beyond our grief and anger. Then, and only then, might we be able to encounter Jesus as he really is and recognize him in the most extraordinary of ordinary actions – the blessing and breaking of bread.

Resurrection Appearances 2: Commissioning

Peace be with you

Luke 24.36–53

Luke 24.36-53   While they were talking about this, Jesus himself stood among them and said to them, 'Peace be with you.' [37]They were startled and terrified, and thought that they were seeing a ghost. [38]He said to them, 'Why are you frightened, and why do doubts arise in your hearts? [39]Look at my hands and my feet; see that it is I myself. Touch me and see; for a ghost does not have flesh and bones as you see that I have.' [40]And when he had said this, he showed them his hands and his feet. [41]While in their joy they were disbelieving and still wondering, he said to them, 'Have you anything here to eat?' [42]They gave him a piece of broiled fish, [43]and he took it and ate in their presence.

[44]Then he said to them, 'These are my words that I spoke to you while I was still with you – that everything written about me in the law of Moses, the prophets, and the psalms must be fulfilled.' [45]Then he opened their minds to understand the scriptures, [46]and he said to them, 'Thus it is written, that the Messiah is to suffer and to rise from the dead on the third day, [47]and that repentance and forgiveness of sins is to be proclaimed in his name to all nations, beginning from Jerusalem. [48]You are witnesses of these things. [49]And see, I am sending upon you what my Father promised; so stay here in the city until you have been clothed with power from on high.'

[50]Then he led them out as far as Bethany, and, lifting up his hands, he blessed them. [51]While he was blessing them, he withdrew from them and was carried up into heaven. [52]And they worshiped him, and returned to Jerusalem with great joy; [53]and they were continually in the temple blessing God.

One of the striking features of Luke's 'commissioning' narrative is how close it draws to stories in the other Gospels while not being exactly the same. Again we are brought back to the recognition that although the Gospels all have different resurrection accounts, they have deep similarities.

The similarities between Luke 24.36–53 and other accounts are:

- Jesus' greeting 'Peace be with you' (also in John 20.20).
- The suggestion that Jesus might be a ghost (also in Matthew 28.9).
- A connection made between Jesus' resurrection appearance and the sending of the spirit (also in John 20.20–23).
- Jesus eating fish (also in John 21.13).
- Jesus showing his hands and his feet (also in John 20.27).
- An expression of doubt/disbelief by the disciples (also in Matthew 28.17).

As has so often been the case, Luke's account functions as a midpoint between John and the other Gospels, enabling us to see how the stories relate to each other.

The big contrast between the accounts of Luke and John is that in John, Jesus breathed the Spirit on his disciples himself, but in Luke this has to wait until Pentecost. It is important to recognize, however, that Luke 24.49 makes it very clear that the Spirit is coming from Jesus, even though it is sent after his ascension: in John Jesus breathed the Spirit on his followers while he was in the same room as them; the implication of 24.49 is that in Luke he sent the Spirit from heaven.

Luke's account has within it an important play on words which is easy to miss in English. The disciples were afraid because they thought they were seeing a 'ghost' in English. In Greek what they thought they were seeing was a '*pneuma*' or 'spirit'. This surely is the point of the whole story. They were frightened because they thought Jesus was a 'spirit'. They should not have been afraid, not only because it was Jesus' resurrected body that they saw but because the true 'Spirit' is not something to be afraid of. At Pentecost they would see the Spirit in all its might but would not be afraid.

John 20.19-23 When it was evening on that day, the first day of the week, and the doors of the house where the disciples had met were locked for fear of the Jews, Jesus came and stood among them and said, 'Peace be with you.' [20]After he said this, he showed them his hands and his side. Then the disciples rejoiced when they saw the Lord.

[21]Jesus said to them again, 'Peace be with you. As the Father has sent me, so I send you.' [22]When he had said this, he breathed on them and said to them, 'Receive the Holy Spirit. [23]If you forgive the sins of any, they are forgiven them; if you retain the sins of any, they are retained.'

The effect of the breathing of the Spirit on the disciples is the same in both John and Luke – they are 'inspired' to follow in Jesus' footsteps proclaiming the gospel to the ends of the earth. John 20.23 can seem an odd ending to this account. Surely Jesus should have sent them to proclaim good news not to forgive sins? The answer is that it is the same thing. Until Jesus forgiveness could only be given by God in the temple. Jesus brought forgiveness out of the temple into the everyday lives of people. He acted on behalf of God forgiving sins and now passes on that authority to his followers. Their authority to forgive sins communicates the good news that they now have to proclaim.

Locked in a house for fear of the Jews

It is worth noting that John's Gospel is the only Gospel that contains this strand of fear of the Jews. In Acts they are also in a room but there they are praying and there is no indication that they fear anyone. The odd thing is that it might have been more sensible to fear the Romans. Accounts in Josephus indicate that the Romans as a rule killed the followers as well as the leader of any Messianic group to ensure that the sedition did not spread. Their apparent lack of interest in Jesus' disciples indicates that they didn't see Jesus as much of a threat.

It may be that the reason for the locked doors was not, in fact, fear of the Jews but to communicate something about Jesus' resurrection body – it was still a body and could eat bread and fish but it was profoundly different and could enter locked rooms at will.

Go and Make Disciples

Matthew 28.16–20

Matthew 28.16-20 Now the eleven disciples went to Galilee, to the mountain to which Jesus had directed them. [17]When they saw him, they worshiped him; but some doubted. [18]And Jesus came and said to them, 'All authority in heaven and on earth has been given to me. [19]Go therefore and make disciples of all nations, baptizing them in the name of the Father and of the Son and of the Holy Spirit, [20]and teaching them to obey everything that I have commanded you. And remember, I am with you always, to the end of the age.'

In Luke and John the key commission takes place in Jerusalem; in Matthew it is in Galilee where they met Jesus on the mountain as instructed. In Matthew mountains are very important and where some key moments in Jesus' ministry take place.

- The sermon on the mount(ain) (5.1).
- The mountain of healing (15.29–30).
- The mountain of transfiguration (17.1).
- The mountain where Jesus talked to his disciples about 'the end' (24.3).
- The mountain of commissioning (28.16).

Some also point to the mountain that the devil takes Jesus to during the temptation narratives (4.8) but this seems to be an altogether different kind of mountain experience.

So important are mountains in Matthew (following on no doubt from the importance of Mount Sinai for Moses) that the occurrence of something on a mountain alerts us to its profound significance, and here the event's significance is vital. The disciples are sent to make disciples of all nations.

This is where faith in the risen Jesus changes the whole landscape of the disciples' lives. Judaism was and remains a non-proselytizing religion. Jews might seek to commend their faith to others but not really to convert them to Judaism. The disciples were sent clearly and explicitly to do this. In the Old Testament the prophets looked forward to a time when the nations would recognize God's glory and flock to his holy mountain (see for example Isaiah 56). Here the resurrection has changed the world so much that now the disciples are sent from the mountain on which they have encountered the risen Christ to take the news of God's glory to the nations themselves.

Doubting

When the disciples met Jesus on the mountain Matthew records that some (or all) of them doubted. Matthew moved directly from this to record that Jesus sent them out to make disciples of all nations. There is no indication that whoever was doubting had stopped doubting before they were sent to make disciples.

One of the big questions surrounding 28.17 is who was doubting? Options include all the disciples, some of the disciples or another group as yet unmentioned. The third option is so unlikely that it can be discarded entirely. It would be odd to introduce a group of people into the narrative whose sole job it was to doubt and go away again. We are left with the question of whether it was some or all of the disciples. The discussion focuses on grammar and how this construction ('hoi de') is used elsewhere in Matthew. My own view is that the verse could refer to all the disciples and so read 'they worshipped but they doubted' but since the effect is not very different from 'they worshipped but some doubted' it is not worth pausing overlong here. The key thing is that some (or all) of the disciples doubted and still were sent out to make disciples.

* * *

Reflection

One of the main excuses that Christians give for not 'making disciples' is that they are not ready. This is an attitude that the churches at least subconsciously encourage. Churches lay on training courses with diplomas and certificates attached so that people can feel trained for the next stage of their ministry. The problem with this is that often it feels as though we need to do one more course, yet another bit of training, and then perhaps in a year or two we may be ready. Jesus seems to suggest another model entirely. Send people out, doubts and all, to make disciples.

This does not mean that we do not need to learn – the word 'disciple' itself means 'learner' – but that we do not need to finish learning before we go. The two processes go side by side, not one in front of the other. We are sent out as we are to 'make disciples' and, because we ourselves are also disciples, as we go we will learn both formally and informally more about who Jesus was and is.

The word 'doubt' is an interesting one. Luke's Gospel says that the disciples did not believe. Matthew says something different. He says they 'worshipped but they (or some of them) doubted'. Doubt is very different to disbelief. Disbelief is the opposite of belief; doubt is the opposite of certainty. The disciples were not sure, but despite that worshipped anyway. Doubt it appears is not a block either to worship or mission.

Feed my Lambs

John 21.1–25

John 21.1–25 After these things Jesus showed himself again to the disciples by the Sea of Tiberias; and he showed himself in this way. ²Gathered there together were Simon Peter, Thomas called the Twin, Nathanael of Cana in Galilee, the sons of Zebedee, and two others of his disciples. ³Simon Peter said to them, 'I am going fishing.' They said to him, 'We will go with you.' They went out and got into the boat, but that night they caught nothing. ⁴Just after daybreak, Jesus stood on the beach; but the disciples did not know that it was Jesus. ⁵Jesus said to them, 'Children, you have no fish, have you?' They answered him, 'No.' ⁶He said to them, 'Cast the net to the right side of the boat, and you will find some.' So they cast it, and now they were not able to haul it in because there were so many fish. ⁷That disciple whom Jesus loved said to Peter, 'It is the Lord!' When Simon Peter heard that it was the Lord, he put on some clothes, for he was naked, and jumped into the sea. ⁸But the other disciples came in the boat, dragging the net full of fish, for they were not far from the land, only about a hundred yards off. ⁹When they had gone ashore, they saw a charcoal fire there, with fish on it, and bread. ¹⁰Jesus said to them, 'Bring some of the fish that you have just caught.' ¹¹So Simon Peter went aboard and hauled the net ashore, full of large fish, a hundred and fifty-three of them; and though there were so many, the net was not torn. ¹²Jesus said to them, 'Come and have breakfast.' Now none of the disciples dared to ask him, 'Who are you?' because they knew it was the Lord. ¹³Jesus came and took the bread and gave it to them, and did the same with the fish. ¹⁴This was now the third time that Jesus appeared to the disciples after he was raised from the dead. ¹⁵When they had finished breakfast, Jesus said to Simon Peter, 'Simon son of John, do you love me more than these?' He said to him, 'Yes, Lord; you know that I love you.' Jesus said to him, 'Feed my lambs.' ¹⁶A second time he said to him, 'Simon son of John, do you love me?' He

---

said to him, 'Yes, Lord; you know that I love you.' Jesus said to him, 'Tend my sheep.' [17]He said to him the third time, 'Simon son of John, do you love me?' Peter felt hurt because he said to him the third time, 'Do you love me?' And he said to him, 'Lord, you know everything; you know that I love you.' Jesus said to him, 'Feed my sheep. [18]Very truly, I tell you, when you were younger, you used to fasten your own belt and to go wherever you wished. But when you grow old, you will stretch out your hands, and someone else will fasten a belt around you and take you where you do not wish to go.' [19](He said this to indicate the kind of death by which he would glorify God.) After this he said to him, 'Follow me.' [20]Peter turned and saw the disciple whom Jesus loved following them; he was the one who had reclined next to Jesus at the supper and had said, 'Lord, who is it that is going to betray you?' [21]When Peter saw him, he said to Jesus, 'Lord, what about him?' [22]Jesus said to him, 'If it is my will that he remain until I come, what is that to you? Follow me!' [23]So the rumour spread in the community that this disciple would not die. Yet Jesus did not say to him that he would not die, but, 'If it is my will that he remain until I come, what is that to you?' [24]This is the disciple who is testifying to these things and has written them, and we know that his testimony is true. [25]But there are also many other things that Jesus did; if every one of them were written down, I suppose that the world itself could not contain the books that would be written.

John is truly a Gospel of the resurrection. Mark has one partial narrative about the resurrection (just the empty tomb); Matthew and Luke three (the empty tomb, an assurance of resurrection appearance and a commissioning), but John has five stories:

- The empty tomb.
- An appearance to Mary.
- An appearance to all the disciples.
- An appearance to Thomas.
- Breakfast on the beach.
- Plus the hint that he could have included lots more.

John's story of breakfast on the beach brings us full circle back to where we began.

Matthew, Mark and John all take us back at the end to the place it all began. In Mark the disciples are told to go to Galilee though we don't know if they make it or not. In Matthew they are told to go and do go, and from there are sent out from the mountain to make disciples. In John they are not explicitly told to go but go anyway back home to the place and activity that shapes who many of them are.

It is surely important that this story rings many bells with Luke 5.1–11. This is the story in which Peter is called in the first place. There as here he has a miraculous catch of fish; there as here Peter's 'sin' is brought into question (Luke 5.8 and John 21.15–17); there as here Jesus says 'Follow me' (Luke 5.10 and John 21.19, though we need to acknowledge that Jesus does not actually say the words 'follow me' in Luke 5). The location, the activity and the miracle all take us back to the beginning once more. The breakfast on the beach summons the disciples back into renewed discipleship of the now risen Jesus, and it summons none as powerfully as it summons Peter.

As many have commented, Peter's threefold invitation by Jesus to love matches and outweighs his threefold denial. The purpose of this conversation is to assure Peter of forgiveness, but the context of a miraculous catch of fish and the calling to 'follow me' takes him right back to the start of his whole journey of discipleship.

Admittedly John's Gospel does not have the miraculous catch of fish at the start of Jesus' ministry. We only find that in Luke, but we have noticed time and time again the overlaps between the different Gospels and it is not beyond the bounds of possibility that John expects his readers to recall that other miraculous catch of fish at the start of Jesus' ministry in Luke. If this is the case, Jesus is taking Peter back to the beginning and calling him again. The slate is clean and the past is forgiven. From there he can be drawn onwards into a future in which his love for the one who is Love can be shown by his care and nurture of Jesus' flock.

The two different words for love

Many people note that in Jesus' exchange with Peter two different words for love are used. Twice Jesus asked whether Peter loved him (using the verb *agapaō*) and twice Peter said that Jesus knew that he loved him (using the verb *phileō*). The last time Jesus asked using the verb *phileō* and Peter replied with the same verb.

Much ink has been spilled by scholars attempting to mine the significance of this. There is no agreement at all. Some think that the difference is vast, vital and significant; others that it is of no significance. My own view is that it probably was significant to John but sadly we cannot now work out what that significance was.

Not only are different words used for love in this passage, Jesus' responses to Peter's declaration of love also contain different words for the care and nurture of his flock.

- Feed my lambs (*boskein arnion*).
- Take care of my sheep (*poimainein probaton*).
- Feed my little sheep (*boskein probation*).

What this seems to point to is that Peter is to go out of his way to care, tend, nurture and feed all those in Jesus' flock both great and small – just as Jesus himself did all through his ministry.

The repetitions in this story emphasize that Peter is called to love, love and love again. Whatever the words he or Jesus used, the beginning, middle and ending of his call as a disciple is a calling out of and into love and John makes sure we keep our gaze firmly on this theme throughout the final story of his Gospel.

* * *

Reflection

John's Gospel carefully guides us to a halt at an ending which feels uncannily like a beginning. This final, beautiful story of love and loving, hints that Peter has taken a long and arduous journey from his first call to 'follow me' through the depths of his own inadequacies and failings and arrived where he started. In this arrival he is helped to see it afresh as though for the first time: this is so often the experience of living the Christian life.

Mrs Alexander, though often so helpful in her hymn writing, did us no favours in declaring that 'he died to make us good' (see 'There is a Green Hill Far Away'). The point is that he didn't die to make us good, he died so that we might be forgiven and might live on in the knowledge of that forgiveness. As Peter discovered, our very best intentions, hopes and dreams cannot ensure that we will be 'good', however we define goodness. What Jesus' death does is to assure us, as Jesus did to Peter on the shore of the lake, that we are forgiven, and we will be forgiven, and that that forgiveness will allow us to arrive again at our beginning and to see it again as though for the first time.

This does not mean that we are constantly going round and round in circles (although it can feel that way), but that when we arrive again at the point where Jesus calls 'follow me', we do follow, this time wiser, this time more humbly, this time more intentionally after the one who continues to call as he did to Peter. Do you love me? – then show it by feeding, nurturing and caring for my sheep.

On the Road to Emmaus

(Based on reflections on Luke 24 above.)

As we walk away defeated and disillusioned,
   Jesus meets us.

As we sling insults at one another,
   Jesus stands alongside.

As we tell our stories of bemusement and betrayal,
   Jesus listens.

As we stand still gloomily
   Jesus waits, ever patient

and then breaks in
   walking with us,
   opening and explaining
   accompanying, comprehending, unpacking

until the moment comes in an ever familiar action
   when we realize that the one for whom we waited
   has been present all along ...

Epilogue

We began our study of the last week of Jesus' life with the question: 'Why did Jesus die?' Now we have completed the journey to the empty tomb and beyond, it is worth returning for a moment or two to this question. The question is no more easily answered now than it was at the start.

Why did Jesus die?

He died because he arrived in Jerusalem at the time of Passover, a time when the Jewish and Roman authorities were more nervous of sedition than at any other time of the year. He died because his conflict with the Jewish authorities became so great that there was no other outcome possible. He died because Judas handed him over to the authorities. He died because no one (including the disciples) tried to intervene in his arrest. He died because Pilate was outmanoeuvred and frightened. He died because the people of Jerusalem got caught up in a group frenzy and lost all sense.

He also died so that the centurion, and all like him, could recognize that he was the Son of God (Mark). He died so that the temple curtain could be torn in two, and God himself could break out of the temple and be at large once more in the world (Matthew). He died precisely because he refused to save himself and by doing so saved us (Luke). He died so that his glory could be revealed throughout the world (John).

All of these – and more – answer the question of why Jesus died. I could go on and on. Paul could offer a large number of his own answers to this question, which would bring sin and atonement much more fully into the answer. But having asked the question and reflected on it deeply, it becomes clear that its real value as a question is that it brings us to the simplest but most mind-blowing of truths.

The really important point is not why Jesus died but *that* he did. As so often, John's Gospel is the one that puts its finger on the deep truth that pulses beneath all our many answers: he died because of love. Jesus died because God's love for the world was so overwhelming that he could not stop pouring it out on the world. Jesus died because his love for his father and for us drove him to express that love in the most sacrificial way possible. Jesus died because his expression of love drove him to reveal the brokenness of the way in which we normally do things, and humanity could not bear the weight or consequences of that revelation.

Why did Jesus die? He died because he loved us – the rest is commentary.

Questions for Bible Study/Lent Groups

I often hesitate to offer questions for Bible study/Lent groups since each group is unique and will want to explore the material in its own way. Nevertheless I am aware that some people value the springboard into discussion that questions can offer, so I suggest some below that may help the conversation to begin on each chapter of the book. Depending on how talkative your group is you may need more questions than there are given below, but they will give you something to start with. I hope you will see these questions as suggestive rather than prescriptive and that you will raise whichever questions have emerged for you and your group in your reflections on the passages.

Some groups will want to study all the Bible passages in each chapter but others will find that too much, so for each chapter I suggest a particular passage you might like to focus on if your group prefers that approach, as well as further questions on the chapter as a whole.

Chapter 1

Focus on Mark 11.1–10

Questions around this passage:

- Do you think 'triumphal entry' is a good title for Jesus' entry into Jerusalem? Can you think of a better title for it?
- What do you think the people who sang 'Hosanna' to Jesus thought was going on?
- What do you think Jesus thought was going on?

Broader questions:

- Does knowing that Psalm 118 lies behind a lot of Mark's account give any fresh insights into your understanding of the events?
- What do *you* think lay behind Jesus' anger in the temple?
- What theme is most important for you in the stories about the anointing of Jesus?

Chapter 2

Focus on Luke 22.8–39 (This passage is chosen because it is the least familiar version and raises interesting questions.)

Questions around this passage:

- Why do you think that Luke has more than one cup in his account?
- Does the last supper change in any way with only one command to 'do this in remembrance of me' in Luke and none in Matthew and Mark?
- If the last supper does remind us of the exodus and looks forward to the Messianic banquet, what themes should be at the top of our minds during a communion service?

Broader questions:

- How important do you think it is for the last supper to be a Passover meal? Discuss some of the problems in timing raised by the different accounts and reflect on what your own view is about the importance of the last supper as a Passover meal.
- Do you think the account of the foot washing in John 13 is the same meal as the last supper?
- What kind of church would we be if we remembered the foot washing as often as we remembered the sharing of the bread and wine?
- Why do you think that Judas decided to betray Jesus? What was he hoping to achieve?

Chapter 3

Focus on Mark 14.32–42

Questions around this passage:

- What do you learn about human vulnerability from (a) Jesus and (b) the disciples in this story? How do the two different types of vulnerability play off each other here?
- Jesus calls God 'Abba' – what do you think is important about the use of 'Father' in prayer? Is it helpful to you?
- In Luke it appears as though an angel is sent to strengthen Jesus to face his agony even more fully. Do you have any reflections on this and the nature of comfort?

Broader questions:

- Why do you think the theme of temptation is so important to Luke?
- Why do you think that John downplays Jesus' agony in the garden?
- How would you compare Judas' betrayal of Jesus with the desertion of Jesus by the other disciples (especially Peter)? Is Judas' betrayal quantifiably worse than that of the others?
- Spend some time reflecting on Peter's response during his trial and Jesus' response during his. Is there any more to learn from these about how to face times of trial?

Chapter 4

Focus on Mark 15.33–41

Questions around this passage:

- What is important for you about the whole earth being covered with darkness at Jesus' death?
- Spend some time reflecting on Jesus' cry of despair 'My God, my God, why have you forsaken me?' Can despair be absolute and yet tinged with hope?

- Why is the temple curtain torn in two do you think? What is important about that for our understanding of Jesus' death?

Broader questions:

- What do you make of the graves also being opened in Matthew?
- What do you think Jesus meant by the words 'Today you will be with me in Paradise'?
- What is important in John's Gospel about Jesus committing his mother to the care of the beloved disciple?
- Do you think the different descriptions of Jesus' actual moment of death are significant in any way?

Chapter 5

Focus on Mark 16.1–8

Questions around this passage:

- Why do you think the women ran away in Mark 16.8?
- Are you convinced that 16.8 is the proper ending to Mark's Gospel? Say why you think what you do.
- Does the fact that Matthew's Gospel has the stone rolled away after the women arrive at the tomb change the narrative significantly?

Broader questions:

- Which is your favourite resurrection story and why?
- Why do you think the disciples didn't recognize Jesus at first?
- Why do you think that John has so many resurrection stories?
- What are your reflections on why the resurrection stories appear to be so different from each other?

For Further Reading

This book has been deliberately short and selective, and some readers will reach the end wanting to explore ideas more. There are, inevitably, a wide range of books you can consult on this part of Jesus' life. In my view some of the best include:

Borg, Marcus J. and John Dominic Crossan, *The Last Week: What the Gospels Really Teach About Jesus's Final Days in Jerusalem*, 1st edn, SPCK Publishing, 2008.

In this book Borg (a Lutheran) and Crossan (a Roman Catholic) join forces – as they do on a number of occasions – to reflect on issues revealed at key moments of Jesus' life. Their interest is particularly in the conflict of allegiances that arose for followers of Jesus in the Roman Empire.

Brown, Raymond E., *A Crucified Christ in Holy Week: Essays on the Four Gospel Passion Narratives*, Liturgical Press, 1986.
—— *A Risen Christ at Eastertime: Essays on the Gospel Narratives of the Resurrection*, Liturgical Press, 1992.

The superb Roman Catholic scholar Raymond Brown offers reflections in these two short books on what he thinks are the key features of Jesus' death and resurrection in the Gospels.

Evans, Craig A. and N. T. Wright, *Jesus, the Final Days: What Really Happened*, ed. Troy A. Miller, Westminster John Knox Press, 2009.

An exploration of what we can know about the history and

archaeology of the last week of Jesus' life from two influential evangelical New Testament scholars.

Some will want to follow their interest in these passages into much more detailed commentaries on each of the four Gospels. Everyone will have their own favourites.

For easy-to-read commentaries it is hard to beat Tom Wright's *New Testament for Everyone Series* published by SPCK.

But for more in-depth approaches I offer my two favourite commentaries on each of the four Gospels below:

Matthew

Davies, W. D. and Dale C. Allison, *Matthew: A Shorter Commentary*, T & T Clark International, 2004.

Nolland, J., *The Gospel of Matthew: A Commentary on the Greek Text*, W. B. Eerdmans/Paternoster Press, 2005.

Mark

France, R. T., *The Gospel of Mark: A Commentary on the Greek Text*, W. B. Eerdmans, 2002.

Myers, C., *Binding the Strong Man: A Political Reading of Mark's Story of Jesus*, Orbis Books, 2008.

Luke

Evans, C. F., *Saint Luke*, 2nd edn, SCM Press, 2008.

Green, J. B., *The Gospel of Luke*, W. B. Eerdmans, 1997.

John

Brown, R. E., *The Gospel According to John*, 2 vols, Yale University Press, 2008.

Lincoln, A., *Gospel According to Saint John*, Baker Book House, 2013.

Biblical Index

For the main discussions of the passages see the pages in bold